MODERN LIFE SKILLS

*How to positively deal with the demands
and challenges of everyday life*

by

Liggy Webb

**Grosvenor House
Publishing Limited**

This book is published by
Grosvenor House Publishing Ltd
28-30 High Street, Guildford, Surrey, GU1 3EL.
www.grosvenorhousepublishing.co.uk

A CIP record for this book
is available from the British Library

ISBN 978-1-78148-551-4

This book is dedicated to my brother and sister

Charles Christie - Webb and Jacky Pearson

Contents Page

Introduction

*Life skills are the abilities for adaptive
and positive behaviour that enable individuals
to deal effectively with the demands
and challenges of everyday life*

The World Health Organization

Life is becoming increasingly challenging and demanding. Stress related illness and emotional "burn out" appear to be rife and sickness absenteeism is costing the economy a colossal amount of money. This, in turn, affects just about everyone, with the tax payer bearing the brunt of it.

There is a great deal of negativity about, with a constant stream of job losses, credit crunches and bankrupt economies. Many businesses and even households are reacting by implementing "austerity measures".

The media seems to almost relish broadcasting, at every opportunity, the latest tales of woe. With so much doom and gloom around, it is little wonder that by 2020 depression will be the second biggest form of global illness according to The World Health Organization.

Our ability to be able to cope with all the constant challenges and changes is essential and cultivating the ability to be positive and adaptable is more important than it has ever been.

The United Nations Educational, Scientific and Cultural Organization (UNESCO) divides life skills into subsets of categories which include the following:

Learning to know (cognitive abilities) which involves decision-making, problem-solving and critical thinking skills.

Learning to be (personal abilities) which involves skills for increasing internal control, managing emotions and handling stress.

Learning to live together (interpersonal abilities) which involves interpersonal communication skills, empathy, co-operation and teamwork.

There is, however, no definitive list of life skills and all of the above includes the psychosocial and interpersonal skills generally considered to be important. The choice and emphasis on different skills will vary according to the individual and circumstances. Though the list suggests these categories are distinct from each other, many skills are used simultaneously in practice. Ultimately, the interplay between the skills is what produces the most powerful behavioural outcomes.

The United Nations' subset of categories for life skills sets out an excellent basis to begin with. There are, of course, other life skills that are required to address a more holistic and balanced approach to modern living that incorporates the physical, psychological and spiritual aspects of life.

In a world that is full of complexity, I have designed this book to be an easy and light read that keeps the key messages clear, simple and concise. It is a tool box for you to dip into whenever you need to and choose from it what works best for you. We are all unique and we all have different strengths and limitations so it's up to you to work out what you need to do to become more confident, resilient and capable.

You will discover a compendium of twenty modern life skills and each one is summarised with the *"Six Steps to Success"*. These are tips to support you in improving the quality of your life and help you to take relevant personal action. Much of the information in this book you may well be familiar with, however it is not what you know, it is what you do with that knowledge that really counts.

Overall the aim of this book is to help you to be able to deal with the demands and challenges of everyday life. This will empower and enable you to survive and thrive and embrace modern living in the happiest, healthiest and most positive way.

Happy Reading

Liggy Webb

Believe in Yourself

Believe in yourself! Have faith in your abilities!
Without a humble but reasonable
confidence in your own powers you
cannot be successful or happy

Norman Vincent Peale

I am a very firm believer that a positive mental attitude will give you the greatest advantage in life and help you to recover from adversity more easily and quicker. Life can be disappointing at times and things can happen that you don't like, however, the way that you choose to respond to these situations is hugely important.

So, before you even begin to explore these key life skills, it is really important that you establish your fundamental relationship with yourself. You need to address your attitude and eradicate as many personal obstacles and negative self limiting beliefs before you can fully benefit from this book.

Fear of failure is one of the greatest limitations people have and worrying too much about what other people think are two of the biggest blockages to personal improvement and growth. Fear of failure is closely related to fear of criticism and rejection.

Remember, successful people look at mistakes as learning experiences, not as failure. If you never made mistakes, how would you learn?

So before we delve into the key life skills here are a few essential bits of advice to help you create the best possible personal foundation:

Take personal responsibility - You are ultimately responsible for everything in your life. Once you accept personal responsibility for that, you will be so much more self empowered and in control of your life and the way that you feel on a day to day basis.

Be positive - Adopt a positive mental attitude. This mind set will give you a far greater advantage in life. Even if something doesn't work out the way you initially wanted it to, at least you will have some valuable learning which may well benefit you in the future. Nothing ventured, nothing gained!

Take action - Action gives you the power to change the circumstances or the situation. You must overcome the inertia by doing something. Ask yourself this question - "What would I do if I knew I could not fail?" Now there is an exciting concept!

Be persistent - Successful people don't just give up at the first hurdle. Successful people keep exploring different approaches to achieve their outcomes until they finally get the results they want. Persistence can very often overcome resistance!

Be objective - You don't need to take failure personally. Failure is not a personality flaw and although sometimes you may not get the results you want, it doesn't mean you are a failure.

Be flexible - Change is the one inevitability in life and something that we may not have any control over. Learning to accept and embrace change and be flexible and open minded will mitigate any stress or fear that you may experience.

Be kind to yourself - If something doesn't work, don't give yourself a hard time; move on and look towards the doors that are just about to open, not at the ones that have just closed.

Learn and grow - You have to be prepared to increase your failure rate if you want to increase your rate of success - Ask yourself the following five questions.

1. What was the mistake?
2. Why did it happen?
3. How could I have prevented it?

4. What did I learn?

5. What will I do better next time?

These words from Thomas Edison who invented the light bulb sum it all up!

> *I have not failed. I've just found 10,000 ways that won't work*

Thomas Edison

Learn and Grow

*Learn from yesterday, live for today,
hope for tomorrow*

Albert Einstein

The ability to be open minded to learning and to actively do something with what you have learnt is really important. We can easily, if we are not careful, amass a great deal of knowledge and information, however, if we don't do something positive with it, then, in some respects, it could be considered a bit of a waste of time! There are many health benefits to learning and more evidence shows the importance of keeping our brain, as a goal seeking mechanism, active, interested and receptive.

It is also useful for us to understand that we are *all* intelligent, however, this can be in different areas – it is not necessarily based on IQ. The theory of multiple intelligences was developed in 1983 by Dr Howard Gardner, professor of education at Harvard University.

It suggests that the traditional notion of intelligence, based on IQ testing, is far too limited. Instead, Dr. Gardner proposes eight different intelligences to account for a broader range of human potential in children and adults. These intelligences are:

Linguistic Intelligence

This intelligence has to do with words, spoken or written. People with high linguistic intelligence are typically good at reading, writing, telling stories and memorising words along with dates. They tend to learn best by reading, taking notes, listening to lectures and discussion and debate.

Logical-Mathematical Intelligence

This intelligence has to do with logic, abstractions, reasoning and numbers. It is often assumed that those with this intelligence naturally excel in mathematics, computer-programming and other logical or numerical activities. They tend to learn best through analysis and practice.

Visual-Spatial Intelligence

This intelligence has to do with vision and spatial judgment. People with strong visual-spatial intelligence are typically very good at visualising and mentally manipulating objects. They tend to learn best through solving puzzles and visually memorising.

Bodily-Kinaesthetic Intelligence

This intelligence has to do with bodily movement. People who have this intelligence usually learn better by getting up and moving around, and are generally good at physical activities such as sports or dance. They tend to learn by actively getting involved and performing and practising.

Musical Intelligence

This intelligence has to do with rhythm, music, and hearing. Those who have a high level of musical-rhythmic intelligence display greater sensitivity to sounds, rhythms, absolute pitch and music. They learn best by listening and creating and practising.

Interpersonal Intelligence

This intelligence has to do with interaction with others. People who have a high interpersonal intelligence tend to be extroverts, characterised by their sensitivity to others' moods and feelings. They learn best by observing and interacting as part of a group.

Intrapersonal Intelligence

This area has to do with introspective and self-reflective capacities. They are usually highly self-aware and capable of understanding their own emotions, goals and motivations. They often have an affinity for thought-based pursuits such as philosophy. They learn best when allowed to concentrate on the subject by themselves.

Naturalist Intelligence

This area has to do with nature, nurturing and relating information to natural surroundings. Those with it are said to have greater sensitivity to nature and their place within it. They learn best by nurturing and growing things as well as recognising and classifying things.

We are all intelligent

We are so conditioned to hold in high esteem the highly articulate or logical people that we don't always appreciate that we are all intelligent in different ways! Dr. Gardner believes that we focus a great deal of our attention on linguistic and logical-mathematical intelligence. He believes that it is important to appreciate individuals who show gifts in the other intelligences who are equally as capable of enriching the world in which we live.

It is useful to be aware of how you learn best and why, so that you can choose the learning channels that work most effectively for you in order to fully maximise your personal potential.

> *Anyone who stops learning is old,*
> *whether at twenty or eighty*

Henry Ford

Changing Your Behaviours

Habits are at first cobwebs
and then they become cables

Spanish Proverb

Over 90% of your daily routine is comprised of various habits that create your behaviours. Most of these habits are performed subconsciously, which means that you are so used to doing them you don't even think about them on a conscious level!

What separates the positive and negative people is that the positive people have habits and behaviours that are conducive to success, whilst the negative people have ones that facilitate failure in their lives.

Remember: you control your habits - they do not control you. Your life is the culmination of all the daily behaviours that you have chosen. You are where you are right now because of the behaviours that you have adopted in the past.

It is important to identify which habits in your life lead to negative consequences and which lead to positive rewards. The difficulty in this sometimes has to do with instant gratification. If you change your habits, on occasions you're not going to see an immediate effect. It is for this reason that people struggle with diets or can't stop drinking, smoking, or spending money because they can't control the instant gratification that is delivered.

Experts in hypnosis and Neuro-Linguistic Programming, which is the art and science of personal excellence, believe that it takes around 21 to 28 days to form the basis of a new habit or behaviour. The time it takes to replace an old one is inconclusive because it depends entirely on the person and how long they have owned it.

As with any newly learned behaviour, you may well experience some internal resistance for the first week or more. This is natural and it's not going to be easy, so you have to mentally prepare for this challenge ahead of time. After you survive this first week, you will find that your new habit and behaviour becomes easier and easier to do and soon you don't even have to think about doing it at all.

Here are a few useful tips to help you change your habits.

Make a record - Just saying you're going to change a habit is not enough of a commitment. You need to actually record what you are going to do.

Make a plan - This will ensure you're really prepared. The plan must include your reasons and motivations for changing, obstacles, triggers, people who will support you, and other ways you are committed to being successful.

Establish strong motives - You have to be very clear why you are changing your habit. If you are doing it for someone else with no real will then you are setting yourself up to fail.

Analyse your obstacles - If you have tried to change this habit before and it hasn't worked, reflect on the reasons why and work out what stopped you from succeeding. Record every obstacle then create a plan of how to overcome them.

Identify your triggers - What situations trigger your current habit? Most habits have multiple triggers. Identify all of them and record them in your plan.

Ask for help - Get your family and friends and co-workers to support you. Ask them for their help, and let them know how important this is to you.

Become aware of self-talk - You talk to yourself, in your head, all the time and may not be consciously aware of what you are programming yourself with. Start listening to those thoughts because they can easily derail any habit, change or goal if you are not careful.

Stay positive - You may well have some negative thoughts and the most important thing is to realise when you are having them and convert them into more positive thoughts. You are totally capable of doing this.

Avoid toxic people - There will always be people who are negative, who try to get you to revert to your old habit. Be ready for them and confront them. You don't need them to try to sabotage you, you need their support, and if they can't support you then avoid them if you can.

Use visualisation - Create a vivid picture, in your head, where you are successfully changing your habit. Visualise yourself doing your new habit. Your subconscious doesn't know the difference between what is real and what is artificial so you will project yourself into the desired state by constantly rehearsing for it.

Reward yourself - When you succeed, you deserve to reward yourself and this will incentivise and motivate you to keep going with whatever you are trying to achieve.

Take "The 30 Day Challenge" - Allow about 30 days to implement a new habit. This will help you to stay focused and consistent and build a routine. This is a round number and the successful outcome will vary from person to person and habit to habit. It is very good starting point.

Bounce back - If you at first you don't succeed, work out what went wrong, make an improvement plan and begin again.

We first make our habits, and then our habits make us

John Dryden

Change Ability

*It is not the strongest of the species
that survives, or the most intelligent, but rather
the one most adaptable to change*

Charles Darwin

Embracing change with an open and positive mind is one of the best bits of advice that I have been given. The only future thing of which we can be absolutely certain is that there will be some degree of change in all of our lives. It is inevitable. You can't stop it! You can't even slow it down or delay it. What you can do, however, with a little knowledge, skill and effort, is to learn how to deal with it. Learning how to consciously direct the changes in your life towards something more positive is most definitely a very important life skill.

Modern living has propelled us into a rapidly and increasingly changing world where the escalating pace of change is far greater today than it has ever been. Every aspect of our lives seems to be changing including the way that we work, the way that we communicate, the way that we shop and eat and, for some, the entire way that we live our day-to-day lives.

It is now quite common for people to change jobs several times. There are those who think nothing of re-locating, not only within their own country but also internationally, taking along with them their entire families. It is also now quite common for people to be married more than once and have more than one family.

Never before have so many people needed to deal with so many life changing decisions, in so many different areas of their lives, on such a consistent and accelerating basis. Indeed, one of the great challenges of our time is the ability to cope with change. As Charles Darwin observed, the ability to be adaptable is indeed key to survival!

At times, the changes may be only minor, however on some occasions, they could have a major impact on our lives. A huge amount of upheaval may well cause anxiety especially if we don't fully understand why the change is happening. It is important,therefore,to attempt to understand why the change is happening and to focus on the potential benefits that it can bring.

We feel much better about the changes that we know or believe are going to make us better off in some way. It is the changes that we are uncertain of, or believe may be detrimental that we get most anxious about. It is important to remember that, even in the most adverse situations, there will always be something positive that comes from it; we may just need to dig deep to find out what it is.

On a very positive note, it is helpful to understand that change is a vital criterion for any form of development and without change there can be no movement or personal growth and development. Certainly it may well cause upheaval, create uncertainty and ruffle a few feathers; however, it can also open many doors to some wonderful possibilities. Making a conscious decision to be positive and open minded about change will help you to deal with some of the more negative aspects that it can conjure up.

Whilst it is useful to be positive, we also need to accept that we are human and we will experience a range of emotions during the change process. Everyone reacts differently and some people thrive on change and see it as stimulating and exciting. In fact they seek out ways in which to change their lives on a regular basis, whether that is through work, relationships, hobbies or even something more dramatic. Some people, however, can become very stressed and agitated and see change as something that totally destabilises their existence.

Understanding how you react to change is important and intelligently managing those emotions will help you to stay more in control.

Elizabeth Kübler-Ross was a Swiss American psychiatrist who was born in 1926 and wrote a book called *On Death and Dying* which included a cycle of emotional states that is often referred to the *"Grief Cycle"*. She observed that this emotional cycle was not exclusive just to the terminally ill, but also to other people who were affected by any change that they perceived with negativity.

Grief Cycle Model

The basic model has been developed by many organisations to help examine the emotional rollercoaster that people experience when they go through change. Some general key stages include:

Shock - This can be the initial reaction when hearing news that may be perceived as negative or unsettling.

Denial - This is very common when people are trying to avoid the inevitable.

Anger - This can be caused by frustration and an outpouring of bottled-up emotion or not clearly understanding why the change is happening.

Bargaining - This is about looking for a way out or attempting to negotiate an alternative.

Depression - This happens when someones perceives the outcome as a negative one.

Acceptance - This is the final stage when people are ready to accept the change and are ready to move forward.

The quickest and easiest way to identify your inner resistance is to observe your own reactions and behaviours as you are experiencing change. So knowledge of this cycle is useful and making notes of how you react in certain situations will help you to understand yourself better.

A strong sense of self awareness will also help you to take personal responsibility and stay more in control. It is up to you how you choose to react to each situation.

Every change will have some impact and sometimes the issue with change is that it has a cluster effect. One change often seems to be followed by several more, and it can feel as though your whole world is changing and that can be quite overwhelming. It is important to get your head around that so that you can deal with it in digestible chunks.

During World War II the British government created the slogan *Keep Calm and Carry On* which has become very popular again recently during challenging times. This seems a very apt personal mantra and certainly from my observation people who deal most successfully with change are those who stay calm and carry on positively influencing and adapting to the changes that occur in their lives.

> *Be the change you want the world to be*

Mahatma Ghandi

Change Ability - 6 Steps to Success

1. Understand why the change is happening

2. Actively seek out the opportunities

3. Be positive and open minded

4. Understand your emotions around change

5. Take responsibility for your reactions

6. Keep calm and carry on

Communication

*The single biggest problem with communication
is the illusion that it has been achieved*

George Bernard Shaw

Effective communication occurs when someone understands you, not just when you speak. One of the biggest pitfalls in communication is when people spend more time trying to make themselves understood than they do to understanding.

Let's face it, when you communicate with someone who is constantly on transmit it can be a bit like talking to the radio! Those who spend too much time in their own little bubble and are not careful, can end up working on the assumption that the other person has understood the message they are trying to get across. This is when successful communication breaks down and becomes an illusion.

It is of course a lot easier to see something from your own perspective and much more difficult to look at it from another person's, especially when we all have such different personalities, backgrounds, ideas, beliefs and values.

Understanding your communication style is very important. Psychometric tests which, translated from Latin, means *measurement of the mind*, are good at helping you to understand your strengths and limitations. One model that I personally favour is based on four personality types and social styles.

Here is a summary of each type and a brief description. It may be worth trying to work out which describes you best. Whilst we cannot cast people into concrete pigeon holes and we may demonstrate attributes of each style, it is likely that one will be the dominant style.

Personality types

Driver - Independent, decisive and determined. Drivers can also be impatient at times and domineering when things don't go the way they want them to. They may feel the need to take control of the situation which others may perceive as controlling and overbearing.

Expressive - Good communicator, expressive and imaginative. Expressives can also talk too much, which other's may perceive as a bit "full on" and overwhelming, especially when the level of detail is more than they require.

Analytical - Thoughtful, disciplined and thorough. Analyticals can also be perfectionists and on occasions get so dragged into the minute detail that they suffer from analysis paralysis. For other people who don't require a huge level of detail to get on with something, it can make them feel impatient and frustrated.

Amiable - Supportive, patient and diplomatic. Amiables can also be bullied by others and lack the ability to be assertive. Because they don't want to offend or upset the status quo they can be hesitant and sit on the fence with a reluctance to make any decisions.

Being aware that we are all different and that we all have strengths and limitations is very important in terms of being able to positively communicate with others. Just because we have a perspective it doesn't necessarily mean that it is the best one and everyone,no matter what their personality style, has something valuable to offer.

Whilst our personalities may stay the same, we can consciously choose to change our behaviours and reactions if we want, to accommodate others' differences and bring about positive outcomes. On stressful days, when you are under pressure, there is a tendency to revert to form and that is when some of these diverse personality styles can clash. For example a dominant driver can get frustrated with the laid back amiable or the imaginative expressive may find the exacting scientific detail that the analytical goes into a bit tedious.

The skill here is to be aware of our limitations and to be mindful about how we react so that our communication doesn't suffer and we can endeavour to look at things from another perspective.

There is a danger that if we are not careful poor communication can lead to negativity, insecurity, back-stabbing and blame. This, in turn, can also affect our stress levels and self esteem, especially when we don't understand something or feel that we have been misled. Communication can also have a very positive effect when it works well and can make people feel valued, respected and even loved.

The development of communication has provided us, in the last few decades, with a whole new range of media including email, instant messaging, the internet and mobile phones. All of these items undeniably have the ability to enhance our communication. However, if misused, these gadgets can create issues and pose problems.

The danger we have is that, with more and more consumer-driven technological toys being created, we are starting to shut out real people in our everyday lives. Whilst social media has its advantages it also has its pitfalls.

Clearly, if we continue to bypass face-to-face communication, our interpersonal skills will suffer as a result. Most human beings need personal interaction. We are social creatures and thrive on cultivating and developing relationships with others. We are now running the risk of alienating ourselves and some of the old traditional means of face-to-face communication are now sadly being lost entirely.

Mobile phones for example can create some real issues. Perhaps you have experienced being in someone's company where they are more interested in checking their text messages or tweeting their latest fan base than giving you the time of day? Perhaps you are even guilty of doing this yourself. I sometimes marvel as I look around in restaurants at the amount of people who sit with their phones next to them on the table.

Being present when you are with someone is key, not just because you will be able to properly listen to what they are saying, it is also important to the other person's self esteem. When we feel we are not being listened to, it can make us feel insecure and lower our self esteem. Active listening is really important.

You talk to yourself subconsciously a great deal and you need to give yourself permission to listen to someone else. This means you literally have to command yourself and say "I am now going to give this person my full attention and really listen to what they have to say".

Avoiding interrupting, jumping to conclusions and filling the gap or making judgements will help you to listen to the whole message, not just to a part of it which is a trap we can all so easily fall into.

Self confidence is also a huge help when communicating so that you communicate your message clearly and assertively. This means getting your message across in a positive, concise and constructive way that works just as well for the person who is on the receiving end.

> *Wise men talk because they have something to say;*
> *fools, because they have to say something*

Plato

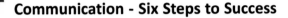

Communication - Six Steps to Success

1. Understand your communication style

2. Positively accommodate other communication styles

3. Be present when you are with people

4. Develop mobile technology etiquette

5. Actively listen and focus

6. Be positive and assertive

Conflict Resolution

Conflict is inevitable, but combat is optional

Max Lucade

It is important to remember that not all conflict is negative. Sometimes a confrontational situation, if it is managed positively, can bring around some very strong results. In fact if we never had any confrontation then progress may never be made!

Conflict is essentially when two or more values, perspectives or opinions are contradictory in nature and haven't been aligned or agreed about. This could indeed be with yourself when you are not living according to your own values or when your values and perspectives are challenged or threatened by someone else.

Conflict is inevitable and we tend to respond in two ways: we either face it or we run away from it. Stop and think for a moment about a time when you have been faced with a conflict situation. Does it make you want to run and hide away or do you prefer to address it head on? Some people positively thrive on conflict situations and almost relish the stimulation it provides. For example, the driver personality that we looked at in the previous chapter may well be in their element, whereas the amiable finds conflict unpleasant and would avoid it at all cost.

What is important to learn, regardless of our initial reaction, is that we must be aware of our natural instincts. Whether we feel like we want to fight or flee when a conflict arises, we can deliberately choose a conflict mode. By consciously choosing a conflict mode we are more likely to productively contribute to solving the problem we are faced with.

Conflict can be really positive because it helps to raise and address problems and can energise the focus to be on the most appropriate issues with a view to resolution and results. Remember, conflict is not the problem; it is when conflict is poorly personally managed that it becomes a problem. Out of control conflict can hamper productivity, demotivate and cause continued conflicts that lead to negative, disruptive and inappropriate behaviours.

In any conflict situation it is better to deal with things calmly and not to become over-agitated. If ever you find yourself in a conflict situation with someone and you are looking to defuse the potential volcano that can erupt, this five - step process that I have designed is a great way to cool down the situation.

The Cool Down Model

Listen - When someone is in a conflict mode they can end up being on transmit due to heightened stress levels. By listening and allowing them to get whatever it is off their chest, they will eventually run out of steam.

Sympathise - This doesn't mean wallowing in a mutual pity party, this means demonstrating that you are in a supportive mode. Simply "I am sorry that you feel this way" can immediately defuse a contentious situation.

Empathise - This is about putting yourself in the other person's shoes and attempting to see the situation from their perspective. There are always three sides to every situation. Your perspective, their perspective and a joint perspective that, may well arrive at together.

Ask questions - Attempt to find out by asking questions what the root of the problem is and what the desired outcome is.

Agree a course of action - It is always good to discuss a balanced course of action that is mutually beneficial and will achieve the best possible outcome. It may take some time to work out what it is, however it is important that all sides are in agreement and support the action plan.

The cool down model is a good way to defuse the situation. Being aware of what can cause conflict is important too. It could well be poor communication or not being informed about changes or simply not understanding another person's motivation. It is important to understand the reasons for decisions. Disagreement about "who does what" and stress from trying to deal with inadequate information or resources can be a real irritation.

Personality clashes are inevitable, because we are all different and it can be frustrating when someone doesn't get our point of view. We can also rub each other up the wrong way and often what we don't like in others is what we actually don't like in ourselves.

In conflict we also need to control our emotions and try to not get angry, aggressive or over sensitive. Anger is often stress in denial and some angry people take pride in their anger and don't want to change; others fail to appreciate the effect it has on themselves and on others. Without a commitment to change, there's not a lot that can be done, anger management is only possible when an angry person accepts and commits to change.

A big factor in persuading someone of the need to commit to change and manage their anger is to look objectively and sensitively with the other person at the consequences of their anger. Often angry people are in denial and put it down to acceptable mood swings and the frustration at the situation as opposed to the way that they are choosing to handle it.

Helping angry people to understand that their behaviour is destructive and negative is an important first step. Most importantly recognising how you handle your own emotions is key.

If you know that you can be hyper-sensitive in certain situations and take things personally, you need to remind yourself of this in moments of high emotion. It may be that we are so involved with the turmoil that is going on within ourselves that we can become defensive and take it out on other people.

Being as objective as possible and focusing on the benefits of resolving conflict is far more positive and conducive to happy living. It is important on occasions to concede that we may not always be right and vice versa. After all, life is rather too short for unnecessary negative confrontation and so much better when we resolve our differences and move on from them in a positive and constructive way.

> *The greatest conflicts are not between two people but between one person and himself*

Garth Brooks

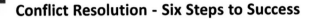

Conflict Resolution - Six Steps to Success

1. Understand the benefits of conflict

2. Use the cool down model to defuse tension

3. Consider the other person's point of view

4. Manage your emotional reaction

5. Seek mutually beneficial outcomes

6. Once the situation is resolved - move on!

Creativity

*Creativity involves breaking
out of established patterns in order
to look at things in a different way*

Edward de Bono

Creativity is a great way for you to explore a wider range of options and to discover new things. It is a useful tool for solving problems or for when you need to explore new and innovative ways of doing things. It is also something that you may need to do to in challenging economic times in order to cut back on some of your overheads and save money.

Creativity is an inborn talent of all human beings and one that can also be developed. It is our creativity that makes us distinct and sets us apart from other animals in this world. When we face challenges and we are not able to solve them in a conventional way, we knowingly or unknowingly seek creative solutions. In fact, in many ways, the more creative we are the more successful we can be.

Whatever our profession is, creativity is something that can make us more successful and can also make our work easier and sometimes more exciting. By being open minded to exploring creative channels we can discover a whole range of options and new doors will open and opportunities will arise.

There are lots of different approaches to creativity. One tip I learnt a long time ago was to carry a small note book with me and to keep it by the side of the bed too. Often inspiration may strike in the night and it is really good to capture those little gems!

Another good way to let the creative juices flow is to take a walk outside. Fresh air is a great stimulant and exercise is a good way to help you to release built up tension so that your minds become more open and your ideas will flow.

Brainstorming or "mind showers" as they are sometimes called these days can be an effective way to generate ideas on a specific topic. This technique is particularly useful when you involve others, and bringing together a group of people with different ideas and perspectives can be very enlightening.

Creative Thinking Tools

There are many creative thinking tools that can be used. One creative technique that I think is really useful to get a good all rounded perspective on a creative idea is Dr Edward De Bono's thinking hats. This is a very popular method where a team can take on different roles and adopt different thinking styles. Each role is identified with a coloured symbolic "thinking hat". By mentally wearing and switching "hats", you can easily focus or redirect thoughts and ideas.

Here is a brief overview of the different thinking styles:

Yellow Hat - This thinking style symbolises brightness and optimism. Under this hat you can explore the positives and probe for value and benefits.

White Hat - This thinking style calls for information known or that may be needed. It is about getting the facts.

Black Hat - This thinking style is about judgment and plays the devil's advocate and challenges why something may not work. Their role is to spot the difficulties and dangers and potentially where things might go wrong.

Red Hat - This hat signifies feelings, hunches and intuition. When using this hat you can express emotions and feelings and share fears, likes, dislikes, loves and hates.

Green Hat - This hat focuses on creativity and the possibilities, alternatives, and new ideas. It's an opportunity to express new concepts and new perceptions.

Blue Hat - This hat is used to manage the thinking process. It's the control mechanism that ensures that the thinking style's guidelines are observed.

Although this works very well with a group of people you can also use it on your own by taking an idea that you have and analysing it from each perspective. For example if you are the eternal sunny optimist, sometimes wearing the darker pessimistic hat can help to give you a more balanced view.

Creativity can be a huge amount of fun, especially when you use methods like this and can help you to explore things that you most likely have never experienced before.

It can, at times, take you out of your comfort zone and challenge you. However it is also very good for you to use creative thinking to keep your brain fresh, stimulated and alert so there are indeed lots of benefits to this approach.

Taking risks for some people can be quite difficult especially for those who like to stay well within their comfort zone and they may well see creativity as change for change's sake. On some occasions they could well be right; however, until you are prepared to take some calculated risks, you will never know if there is a better or more efficient way of doing something.

We live in a very fast paced life and sometimes we don't allow ourselves time to think. Giving a lot of free time for your mind is an excellent approach. Putting some of your worries and tensions aside for some time every day is very important.

When we are relaxing, the mind is actually working and putting together things that we were thinking of throughout the whole day. It will come out with creative solutions only if we give it enough time and rest. Always pondering over endless problems keeps our minds occupied and prevents creativity. So managing your stress levels and de-cluttering your mind is key.

Getting stuck in one way of thinking and trying repeatedly the same methods is a common phenomenon among us. It is also the best way to go a little bit mad! If you have been churning something over and over in your mind and can't seem to find a solution, attempt to stop thinking about it, relax and get engaged in something else for a while. You may well find that when you attend to the problem after some time, your mind views the problem in a different way and a solution may come along straight away!

Creativity is inventing, experimenting, growing, taking risks, breaking rules, making mistakes, and having fun

Mary Lou Cook

Creativity - Six Steps to Success

1. Be open minded and receptive to exploring creativity

2. Always carry a small notebook with you

3. Go for a walk in the fresh air to stimulate your mind

4. Brainstorm with others and share ideas

5. Use "De Bono's Thinking Hats" as a creative thinking tool

6. Step out of your comfort zone and take some risks

Decision Making

Decision is like a sharp knife that cuts straight and clean, indecision a dull one that hacks and tears and leaves ragged edges

Graham Gordon

We have to make decisions every day of our lives and I think that this quote can sum up the way indecision makes us feel. Some decisions are relatively straightforward and others are definitely more difficult. Simple decisions usually need a simple decision-making process. Difficult decisions, however, typically involve a whole host of complex issues.

Very often there is uncertainty where many facts may not be known and you may have to consider many interrelated factors. There are decisions, too, that have high-risk consequences, and the impact of the decision might have a high implication for you or for others.

Every given situation has its own set of uncertainties and consequences, and anything that involves interpersonal issues can often be challenging as it difficult to predict how other people could respond.

All in all decision making can be quite a stressful process!

The best way to make a complex decision is to use an effective process. A systematic approach will also lead you to consistent, high-quality results, and can improve the quality of almost everything we do. A logical and systematic decision-making process will help you to address the critical elements that result in a good decision. By taking an organised approach, you're less likely to miss important facts and you can build on the approach to make your decisions better in the future too.

Making Decisions

Here is a critical path that you can take when assessing each situation when you need to make a decision about something:

1. Identify your decision and establish your objective

2. List the various options that you have available

3. Gather as much information as you need on all of them

4. Conduct a risk analysis and weigh up the pros and cons of each

5. Analyse your own strengths and limitations

6. Select the best option and develop a plan of action

7. Implement your decision and stick with it

If you have to involve other people it is so important to involve the right people and allow other opinions to be heard. It is also important when you make any decision to also be aware of the implication that it will have on others .Whilst you may be prepared to take a gamble, if you are putting others in a difficult position it is important to take that into consideration and act with integrity. Make sure, that you are asking the right questions and challenge yourself.

Being creative will help you too, as the basis of creativity is all about thinking about things from a different perspective. So it is a great way to beginning the exploration process of what options you have available to you.

The more options you consider, the more comprehensive your final decision will be.

When you generate alternatives, you force yourself to dig deeper, and look at the problem from different angles. If you use the mindset of "there must be other solutions out there", you are much more likely to make the best decision possible and not miss anything.

When you're satisfied that you have a good selection of realistic alternatives, then you'll need to evaluate the feasibility, risks and implications of each choice.

In decision making, there's usually some degree of uncertainty, which inevitably leads to risk. By evaluating the risk involved with various options, you can determine whether the risk is manageable. Risk analysis helps you look at risks objectively. It uses a structured approach for assessing threats, and for evaluating the probability of events occurring.

There will always be some element of risk attached to everything we do as we cannot predict the outcome. Sometimes we will make decisions that we may well look back on and feel that perhaps another approach may have been better. That is life! We cannot expect to get it right all the time. Also if we did, how would we learn? If we get caught in a paralysing loop of fear because we don't want to make a mistake or take a risk the chances are we would never get anywhere. Sometimes you just need to take a leap of faith.

So once you have evaluated the alternatives, the next step is to choose between them. With all of the effort and hard work that goes into evaluating alternatives and deciding the best way forward, it's easy to forget to "sense check" your decisions. This is where you look at the decision you're about to make dispassionately, to make sure that your process has been thorough, and to ensure that common errors haven't crept into the decision-making process.

Once you've made your decision, it's important to explain it to those who may be affected by it, and involved in implementing it. The more information you can give to people about why you made a certain decision, the better. One of the key benefits of taking the systematic approach to decision making is that you will be able to analyse and evaluate your decision making process which will, in turn, make it easier to communicate. If you need support of others they will also feel more reassured that you have given consideration to your actions. This will be so helpful to you and to those around you and very much appreciated. As with any change, the more information you provide the better.

This will also give you personal reassurance that you have thought something through without making a knee-jerk decision.

One you have made your decision, stick with it, accept that you have made the best decision based on all the information that you had at the time. Deliberation or indecision will hamper your progress, so go for it and trust in a positive outcome.

Yes of course there may well be occasions where you have to accept that you could have done it differently or even better. Give yourself the best possible chance with the best possible information and at least you will know that you did something with your best possible intention and effort!

> *In any moment of decision, the best thing you can do is the right thing, the next best thing is the wrong thing, and the worst thing you can do is nothing*

Theodore Roosevelt

Decision Making - Six Steps to Success

1. Establish a decision making process
2. Identify who else may be involved
3. Create a broad range of options
4. Analyse the pros and cons of each option
5. Develop an implementation plan
6. Be positive about your decision and stick with it

Empathy

*People will forget what you said,
people will forget what you did, but people
will never forget how you made them feel*

Bonnie Jean Wasmund

To truly master the art of developing a positive bond with other people, empathy is a very important life skill. It is the emotional process that builds connection between people. It is a state of perceiving and relating to another person's feelings and needs without blaming them, giving advice or trying to fix their situation which, on occasions, can be very tempting to do. The danger with this is that we can superimpose on to them our own solution which may not always work for the other person!

To empathise and understand another individual is an intuitive act where you give complete attention to someone else's experience and push aside your own issues. To be truly empathetic is about helping another person feel secure enough to open up and share their experience. In order to do this, they will need to trust you. By being empathetic and understanding, you will help the other person feel that they are not entirely isolated in their predicament and you can provide them with a safe haven to recover and grow stronger, knowing they have a supporter.

Just to clarify, empathy is different from sympathy. When someone is sympathetic, whilst it also implies support, it is a feeling that is more fuelled by pity and you will usually maintain an emotional distance from the other person's feelings. An empathetic and understanding approach is more about truly sensing or imagining the depth of another person's feelings. It implies feeling *with* a person, rather than feeling sorry for them.

Empathy is a translation of the German term *Einfühlung*, meaning to feel as one with. It implies sharing the load, or "walking a mile in someone else's shoes", in order to appropriately understand the other person's perspective. This can take time and patience.

Having a rich capacity for empathy and understanding is also a wonderful quality if it is used in the right way. Once you understand someone you can use that understanding to help them and to help them heal themselves. If you reject the skill of empathy, you reject the ability to really understand your fellow humans as well as you could. Here is a critical path that you can follow to develop your empathy skills.

Developing Empathy

1. Give the person you are talking to your undivided attention
2. Be objective and avoid pre-conceived judgments
3. Observe and listen to the emotion behind the words
4. Avoid interrupting even though you may want to
5. Be careful not to jump to an early conclusion
6. Communicate that you understand and want to be supportive
7. Ask questions where relevant to help the person gain some clarity

To really increase your ability to empathize it is important too, that you start with yourself. Pay close attention to your emotional state and what makes you feel positive and negative. This is a good basis from which to understand that people have different emotional responses to just about everything.

We are very lucky in the developing world that we have more opportunity to mix cross culturally and learn more about people from a wide range of backgrounds. We can get to know people from all ages, ethnicities, sexual orientations, socio-economic backgrounds and levels of physical ability. The more people you get to know, the more experiences you will have to draw on and this can really help you to increase your ability to empathize.

Fostering empathy in those around you is a good thing to do and looking for the similarities between yourself and others is an interesting and sometimes challenging exercise. When you simply focus on the differences between yourself and other people, it is much more difficult to understand others.

It is useful as well to practice taking on another's perspective. On occasions you may feel that your perspective is the only viewpoint available, however this is simply not true. Educate and condition your mind to be more open to the perspectives of others and immerse yourself in a different viewpoint. Not only will this improve your ability to be more empathetic it will help you to grow.

One thing to be aware of is that unless you can extend compassion, empathy, and understanding to yourself then you won't be able to genuinely extend it to others. Not having authentic empathy and understanding for yourself can leave you feeling lonely or alienated and it can also lead to feelings of isolation and depression. Being kind and gentle to yourself is very important.

If you are not in touch with your own feelings you are likely to have an inhibited sense of conscience. You will find it hard to relate to another person's suffering and also find it very difficult to connect and relate, which, in turn, will make others feel inadequate and even potentially angry. I am sure we have all experienced people who have little ability to empathise and will label a sensitive person as "too sensitive". The question I would ask would be "too sensitive for whom?".

For those who have the ability to empathise, it is important also to try to understand people who are unable to, and to try to understand that these people may be dealing with some psychological pain of their own and a coping mechanism is to shut their feelings down internally and externally.

The ability to positively empathise and understand is indeed to extend the hand of human kindness.

Wouldn't it be great if we could all do this and seek to understand rather than always to be understood. Wouldn't it be a much happier and healthier world if we developed our ability to show sensitivity to other peoples' thoughts and feelings and learned to be more compassionate and empathetic?

> *If there is any one secret of success, it lies in the ability to get the other person's point of view and see things from his angle as well as your own*

Henry Ford

Empathy - Six Steps to Success

1. Get in touch with your own feelings

2. Understand the range of emotions people can experience

3. Be genuinely interested in what others feel

4. Be willing to put yourself in the others person's shoes

5. Be open minded to all perspectives

6. Extend the hand of human kindness

Feedback

Feedback is the breakfast of champions

Ken Blanchard

Feedback is the food of progress and, whilst it may not always taste great, it can be very good for you. The ability to provide constructive feedback to others is really helpful in terms of helping them to tap into their personal potential and can certainly help to forge really positive and mutually beneficial relationships.

From your own personal perspective any feedback that you receive is free information and you have the choice entirely whether you want to take it on board or not. It is a great service with regards to helping you to discover things you don't know about yourself and very useful in terms of helping you to get a different perspective.

Some people find it very challenging to accept feedback and can get very uncomfortable around giving it, even when it is positive.

So much of it has to be around how it is delivered. There are occasions where I have felt patronised when someone has delivered feedback; however, the key skill here is to see beyond the delivery technique and focus on the quality of the message.

Remember feedback is a gift. It is free information that you can do anything you like with.

In terms of being good at giving feedback, it is really important to first of all ask yourself: will this feedback be useful and, actually, can this person do anything about it? If the answer to both those questions is yes then it is constructive. Following a process will be helpful and this is a good formula

Feedback Formula

⇨ Tell someone what they did

⇨ Explain the effect that it had

⇨ Help them to explore alternative ways of doing it if it is negative

⇨ Reinforce the continuation of doing it if it is positive

Also it is good to get a balance of positive and negative. Sometimes in the workplace or in relationships with loved ones we spend a lot of time focusing on what someone isn't doing well and not enough time celebrating the things that people do well so that they keep on doing them and feel good about themselves.

Giving feedback isn't just a great way to help people around you perform better and achieve more. If it is done properly, it will also make them feel better!

Here are some key pointers when delivering feedback.

Choose your timing - Tactful feedback isn't shouted to a person across a room at the end of the day. It is important to dedicate some quality time for the sole purpose of giving feedback, whether it's just a minute or part of a formal meeting. Properly announce your intentions by asking "I would like to give you some feedback on something. Would that be all right and when is a convenient time for you?"

Be honest - The purpose of giving feedback is to align the person's perception of their behaviour with your observation. If your idea of feedback is to spoon feed half-truths in an attempt to shift their behaviour to suit your ends, you may only be making things worse. An honest and assertive approach will create a "win-win" outcome.

Make it digestible - If feedback is the food of progress as I mentioned, sometimes it may be good for someone; however, it may not always taste nice! Use the "compliment sandwich" or more exotic varieties. A compliment sandwich is where you offer a compliment followed by a constructive point, and closed with a further positive feedback point. The theory is that this approach will help the conversation end on a more positive note.

Listen to your own voice - The tone of your voice can communicate as much, if not more, than the words you choose. If there is a hard critical edge to your voice it will have an effect on the feedback you deliver.

Keep eye contact - Giving feedback can be challenging so eye contact is essential to maintain trust and helps both of you stay focused and it communicates sincerity. If you're working on something, stop what you're doing and look at the person you're speaking to. Be totally present.

Avoid hurting anyone's feelings - Use a softened start-up followed by a gentle suggestion. For example you could say, "I really like the way you talk to your supervisor; you would get a better response from your team members if you spoke to them in the same way".

Talk about the behaviour, not the person - This is really important. Feedback is not about insulting someone's behaviour, it's about telling them how to be better and achieve better outcomes.

Let it go - Once you have given your feedback, don't keep feeling the need to repeat yourself, you need to then allow the person to absorb the information and take action. If you have to ask someone to do something four times, I can promise you that the person in question has heard what you have to say and has most likely decided not to take on board the feedback. If you've reached an agreement or agreed to disagree, let it go and move on.

Sometimes people won't necessarily immediately recognise how positive some feedback can be. It may take a while for them to reassess and to later recognise the positive impact it has made on their lives.

Now let's turn this around and examine what it is like to be on the receiving end of feedback. To receive honest, constructive feedback is much like receiving a gift, whether we think so or not at the time. The challenge is to receive feedback with an open mind and learn from it, and disregard our natural instinct to defend ourselves or our actions.

As Eleanor Roosevelt said: *"No one can make you feel inferior without your consent."*

Giving and receiving constructive feedback needn't be the anxiety filled experience that sometimes we create in our minds. By developing the attitude that feedback is a gift in disguise it will enable you to be more positive and more confident about this life skill as a development tool. It will help you to tap into your undiscovered and unleashed potential and also help you to help others to achieve more and to become more successful. Feedback is a wonderful tool and used constructively can open so many doors to so many amazing possibilities. Feedback is indeed the food of progress.

> *Champions know that success is inevitable; that there is no such thing as failure, only feedback. They know that the best way to forecast the future is to create it*

Michael J Gelb

Feedback - Six Steps to Success

1. View feedback as the food of progress

2. Be responsive and open minded

3. Use the feedback formula

4. Focus on behaviour nor personality

5. Only feedback something that can be changed

6. Make feedback a positive experience

Goal Setting

Man is a goal-seeking animal.
His life only has meaning if he is reaching
out and striving for his goals

Aristotle

Setting goals is a great way to keep ourselves motivated and having something to look forward to can help you to feel more inspired and positive. These goals do not have to be huge scary milestones that we set ourselves. In fact it is very important that when we set ourselves goals that whilst we may want to stretch ourselves we ensure that they are achievable.

Goals unlock your positive mind and release energies and ideas for success and achievement. Without goals, you simply drift and flow on the currents of life. With goals, you fly like an arrow, straight and true to your target. Setting goals will give you direction, purpose and a focus in your life. It also helps you to take more control over what happens to you.

There are lots of benefits to setting goals. First and foremost, they help you to develop clarity which is the first step to helping you achieve what you want in life.

If you have clear goals and focus on them, you will get more of what you do and want and less of what you don't want.

When you are clear about where you want to go, you can set up a plan with some steps and actions of how to get there. This increases your efficiency because you are working on what is really important. When you work on what's important, you will accomplish more than you ever expected. You will get what you really want in life, rather than settling for "whatever comes your way".

As you set and reach you goals, you will in turn become more confident in your ability to do what you say and get what you want in life. Success most definitely breeds more success. In my view people can make their own luck!

One of the main reasons that your brain needs goals is that it behaves as a goal-seeking mechanism, similar to a precision-guided missile. As these missiles fly, they continually make small adjustments and corrections to their trajectories to realign themselves to their target.

Your brain also works in a similar way. Dr Maxwell Maltz, author of the classic *Psycho-Cybernetics*, said that human beings have a built-in goal-seeking "success mechanism" that is part of the subconscious mind.

This success mechanism is constantly searching for ways to help us reach our targets and find answers to our problems. According to Maltz, we work and feel better when our success mechanism is fully engaged and going after clear targets.

All we have to do to use this mechanism is to give it a specific target. Without one, our success mechanism lies dormant, or worse, pursues targets we didn't consciously choose.

It is also useful to think of a time when maybe we haven't felt so good, perhaps a time when we have been a bit lost and depressed. The likelihood is that it will be a time when you have had nothing to look forward to and felt that there was a lack of hope and direction in your life. This can be a reminder and a motivator that having a goal is a positive thing and everyone needs a good reason for getting up in the morning!

Being creative and looking for ways to make progress in your life will bring about ways of discovering new things and will keep you stimulated and interested. Until you start to explore new possibilities you will never find out what works for you. We are so fortunate that we have so much available to us these days. Goal setting is a very good way of distilling what it is important to you.

Incredibly only 3% of people have proper written goals. According to research people who actually make a record of their goals accomplish 80% more than those who don't. That's an astounding difference, isn't it? So it is well worth creating a personal action plan.

A common acronym in objective and goal setting is the SMART acronym. You may well have heard of this already.

The SMART acronym is used to describe what experts consider to be "good" objective or goal statements because they contain most of the essential ingredients. Out of all the formulas I have come across for objective and goal-seeking, it is by far the best and the most easy to apply and stick to.

The SMART acronym has several different variations depending on who you ask. However, I think it is useful to look at all of them because it provides a well-rounded goal statement and then you can choose which works best for you.

Smart Objectives and Goals

S - Specific & significant
M - Measurable, motivational, methodical & meaningful
A - Action-oriented & achievable
R - Realistic, relevant & recorded
T - Time-bound & tangible

If you would like a complimentary copy of an electronic SMART action plan email support@modernlifeskills.com

The key with goal setting is to assertively take control of what we want and to identify exactly what it is that we really want to achieve with a clear understanding of why we want to. Very often we can set ourselves goals that we are not really committed to because we don't really understand how we will benefit from the final outcome. This ultimately is what will keep you motivated when you go off track, which will happen from time to time. So a good solid reminder of what you are doing it is so important.

Stickability when you set goals is the name of the game and I have always thought that goal setting is a great way of determining whether you really want something or not! It takes about 21 – 28 days to form a new habit and on some occasions up to 3 months to change an old habit. Setting yourself a 3 month plan is a good start. When you have a plan it is also good to share it with a friend or a colleague who can help you stay on track.

The benefits of goal setting and goal achievement are numerous. There is a whole world of possibility out there and setting goals will allow you to become more empowered and altogether more responsible for your own future and personal success. It will also help to boost your self-esteem and self-confidence when you make progress which, in turn, has many physical, emotional and mental health benefits.

> *I don't want to get to the end of my life and find that I have just lived the length of it. I want to have lived the width of it as well*

Diane Ackerman

Goal Setting - Six Steps to Success

1. Positively embrace the benefits of goal setting

2. Be clear about why you are trying to achieve something

3. Use the SMART formula Set goals that you are committed to

4. Ensure that you record your personal action plan

5. Share your plan with someone else

6. If it is important to you – Stick with it!

Healthy Living

The greatest wealth is health

Virgil

It is interesting the way that so many people can be very focused on saving money for the future and not even think about the investment that they make in their health and bodies on a day to day basis. We need to think of our bodies as a pension fund and make some healthy investments sooner rather than later.

World health statistics are currently very disturbing, with the World Health Organization reporting that one in three adults worldwide have raised blood pressure, a condition that causes half of all deaths from strokes and heart disease. One in ten people have diabetes. In the last thirty years obesity has doubled!

With so much pressure now on our health services it is becoming more and more important that you take more care and responsibility for your own wellbeing.

What are your energy levels like? Do you refuse the snooze button on your alarm clock and wake up full of beans with a "ready to get up and get going attitude " in the morning? Are you able to maintain high levels of energy throughout the day? Perhaps like so many people, you rely a lot on caffeine or sugar to keep you going. Do you have much energy left at the end of the day or do you crash in front of the television feeling exhausted?

During the day you are bound to go through stages of feeling up and down with changing energy levels .Your bodies go through a repeating energy cycle (ultradian rhythms) every 90 to 120 minutes. The implications are that we can only do solid work for up to about 90 minutes at a time and then we need a break or to at least switch off and do something a bit easier or lighter.

The real skill in managing your health and daily energy is to work on the more difficult things when you are alert and focused and to work on the easier things when you're feeling lower in energy. To maximise your energy, you need breaks. Taking a short mini break every ninety minutes is a good idea. If you are desk bound get up and have a good stretch.

One good tip is to get up and get going in the morning. The brain, as a goal seeking mechanism, likes to get going once we are awake so, if we refuse the snooze on our alarm, we will embrace our day already more energised.

Typically, everything we do either builds or takes away from our energy reserves. Effective time usage depends on looking after multiple sources of energy. These include physical, emotional and mental energy.

Exercise is an excellent energiser. I saw a strap-line once that said: "Energy – the more you give the more you get" which, I thought, sums up exercise very well. People who exercise regularly are likely to live longer and enjoy a better quality of life. It is very important for your heart.

Regular exercise also improves mental and emotional health. The chemicals and hormones that are released in the brain through exercise can help deal with stress, promote wellbeing and provide us with more sustainable energy. If you are challenged with depression, research has shown that thirty minutes of exercise a day can be as effective as a mild anti-depressant. So get up and get going.

Get Active

⇨ **Go for a walk each morning and each evening** - Even if it's just for 15 minutes before and after work.

⇨ **Take the stairs** - Climbing stairs is actually a great workout especially for your legs and bottom.

⇨ **Give someone a massage** - This is one of the best ways to work with your hands.

⇨ **Ride your bike to work** - If it's not too far away this is a great way to get some extra exercise

⇨ **Go swimming** - Swimming is just about one of the best ways to exercise and it is a great aerobic workout no matter what your physical shape is

⇨ **Stretch each day** - Stretching helps to prevent muscle cramps and alleviates back pain as well as reducing stress.

⇨ **Volunteer** - Whether it's distributing food to the needy, helping elderly people, or participating in a fundraiser for a worthy cause in your community.

Learning to relax and let go of worry and stress at the end of the day is key. By keeping a clear conscience so that you can relax in the knowledge that you have stuck to your values and principles is one way of being able to clear your mind of anxiety.

Stress can affect sleeping patterns, and poor quality sleep will most definitely affect energy levels. If you are worried about something, it can often be on your mind even when you try to forget about it. This may cause sleepless nights or bad dreams. You may find it difficult getting to sleep or you may wake up a few times during the night. This can also make you tired and groggy the next day.

With regards to mental energy, it is important to be careful with what we feed our minds as negative thinking can be a real drain and we can be our own energy saboteurs. We need to learn to switch off so that our mind and body has time to recharge, so some kind of meditative activity would be good, even if it just going for a walk, having a hot bubble bath or spending more time with loved ones.

Healthy eating with plenty of vegetables and fruit and being light on the fats and sugars is important, as is making sure you are hydrated by drinking sufficient water. Breakfast is the most important meal of the day as it sets you up after a good night's sleep. A good slow carbohydrate-releasing breakfast like porridge is excellent for sustaining energy levels. Sugar-rich food will give you a quick energy fix but will leave you feeling even more tired later on. Keeping raw vegetables and fresh fruit as energy boosting snacks is a far better habit to get into.

It is really important to reduce caffeine and alcohol. Two cups of coffee a day is sufficient, any more and it will affect your energy levels and is not recommended for good health.

Alcohol needs to be within the government guidelines which suggests 14 units a week for women and 21 for men. It is worth being aware that a large glass of wine can be 3 units!

One of the very best things you can do is to drink lots of water which will keep your body hydrated, flushing out toxins and controlling your appetite. Drinking two litres of water throughout the day is one of the healthiest habits that you can have and I highly recommend this for energetic and healthy living.

> *And what is a man without energy?*
> *Nothing - nothing at all*

Mark Twain

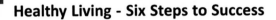

Healthy Living - Six Steps to Success

1. Refuse the snooze on your alarm

2. Always eat breakfast

3. Exercise for 30 minutes every day

4. Take breaks every 90 minutes

5. Reduce caffeine and refined sugar

6. Drink 2 litres of water a day

Impact and Influencing

Think twice before you speak, because your words and influence will plant the seed of either success or failure in the mind of another

Napoleon Hill

Making a positive impact and having the ability to influence people is a very powerful life skill to possess. More and more, in the competitive world in which we live, having the confidence to stick your head above the parapet and get noticed is very helpful, not just in a work environment but also on a personal level.

The key is to make the best impact that you can have on people's lives and to be conscious that all of your actions bear consequences. Treating people how you would want to be treated is very important and having respect for your fellow man is indeed a virtue.

You can actively seek out ways to make a positive impact and, by generating enthusiasm and energy, you can add value and help influence others to feel good about themselves. Self-confidence (and remember there is a fine line between confidence and arrogance) will breed confidence in others. The greatest leaders in the world have one thing in common and that is a sense of purpose and self-belief.

We have already covered self belief at the beginning of this book and identified that you need to believe in yourself before you can expect anyone else to. So that is the very first step to making a positive impact.

Making a positive impact however is not just about how you initially come across, it is also about developing a positive and sustainable rapport with the other person. Listening, empathising and cultivating trust will most certainly help you to create a better connection which will ensure that people are responsive to you. Here are few tips on how to make some good impressions

Positive Impact

1. Work on developing your self confidence by increasing your self- awareness and being aware of your strengths and limitations.

2. Communicate with people in an assertive manner by getting your message across in a way that is positive and constructive.

3. Be aware of your body language and make sure that it is open.

4. Listen to what other people say and create empathy and trust so that you can connect more easily.

5. Be enthusiastic and generate positive energy. This can be contagious.

6. Look at people and talk with your eyes

7. Smile - it is a universal language

8. Be genuine and be the best version of who you are

So, once you have made a positive impact, you will find it far easier to influence and persuade people because they will already be on your side.

Influencing is an important skill to have and we all approach this in different ways. We looked at the four communication styles in the chapter on communication and this is a good basis in helping you to understand what your strengths and limitations are. It will also help you to be aware of the way in which you may go about influencing people and the way in which people may respond.

If you want to be a really successful influencer you need to understand who you are dealing with and what will work best for them otherwise you may appear too aggressive or not assertive enough! Also, people are turned on in different ways so learning what motivates someone will be very helpful. This is where listening and observing rather than racing in full throttle will be the best approach.

It is also important that you establish first of all what you are trying to achieve. If you are unclear about your own intentions or direction, it will just confuse other people and they will, in turn, lose confidence in where you are trying to take them. Time for many these days is of the essence and time wasters are never popular!

Influence, by definition, is about having a power and power over others, so it is important that you use this power with integrity and due diligence. One of the key skills when influencing is to listen actively and make sure that you have all the facts around you so that you are well informed and are responsible when you are leading people, in the direction that you want to take them and toward the outcomes that you want to achieve. Demonstrating empathy and understanding will also help to get people on your side and make them feel far more part of the process, as opposed to being railroaded into something that they may resent you for later.

A good amount of planning and preparation will help to keep you focused and also demonstrate to those around you that you are in control and that you know what are you are doing. If an idea or suggestion has been well thought through it will have far more gravitas.

Openness and honesty about the merits and pitfalls of a suggestion can be very positive too, as this provides a reality check and acknowledges and pre-empts any doubts that anyone may have. They will be more receptive to being influenced if the pros and cons have been weighed up and they have all the facts.

The more you make someone involved and part of the process, the more they will be on your side. Also remember one of the key skills of influencing is the enthusiasm you convey when delivering any message. A passion, energy and strong belief in what you are trying to achieve can be contagious and the best way to positively impact on and influence others.

Do be mindful however that if you are a very enthusiastic person you do need to be a bit careful that you don't whip people into a frenzy of enthusiasm without a support plan. Very creative and expressive people can on occasions get so carried away with an idea that in their own minds has already become a reality. The danger with this is that you disappoint people and when people feel let down too often they will stop being receptive to any influence that you may have had with them.

> *You don't have to be a "person of influence" to be influential. In fact, the most influential people in my life are probably not even aware of the things they've taught me*

Scott Adams

Impact and Influencing - Six Steps to Success

1. Believe in yourself and your abilities

2. Be assertive and develop trust

3. Treat people how you would like to be treated

4. Manage your enthusiasm appropriately

5. Plan ahead and prepare yourself

6. Be genuine and influence with integrity

Life Balance

I've learned that you can't have everything and do everything at the same time

Oprah Winfrey

This quote from Oprah seems to sum up quite well the way that we can approach our lives if we are not careful. Sometimes we can end up wanting to do everything, have everything and then we complain and get stressed out by the fact that we just don't seem to have enough time!

This is where we need to take hold of our lives and make some choices. One of the big conundrums of modern living is the volume of choices we have available to us and this in itself can present us with some challenges. Finding a balance in life, in my opinion, is the ultimate life skill and the one that is the most difficult to master.

The term *work-life balance* has been bandied about since the 1970's. I think the term *life balance* is more appropriate because work is part of our whole lives as are our homes, relationships and fulfilling our own additional ambitions.

Many people spend more time at work than they do at home and more time with work colleagues than with friends and family so work is a huge part of their lives.

Work is fast becoming the way in which we define ourselves. It is now answering some of the traditional questions like "Who am I?" and "How do I find meaning and purpose in my life?" Work is no longer just about economics; it's about identity. About fifty years ago, people had many sources of identity: religion, class, nationality, political affiliation, family roots, geographical and cultural origins and more. Today, many of these, if not all, have been superseded by work.

An alarming amount of absenteeism in the workplace is now stress-related and it is clear that problems caused by stress have become a major concern to both employers and employees. Symptoms are manifested both physiologically and psychologically.

It is now more important than ever that people learn to manage their lives so that they create a better balance and reduce unnecessary stress which in turn will promote better long-term health and wellbeing.

The idea of life balance is further complicated by the fact that today's workforce is more culturally diverse and also made up of different generations, each with its own set of priorities. Additionally, businesses are in various stages of their own life cycles. Instead of looking for a generic, standardised concept of life, we need to understand that it is our own responsibility to make sure that we implement personal strategies that help us to get a better perspective on how we can better balance our time and energy.

Here are a few tips on how you can achieve a better balance

Get up and get going - This is such a good way to start the day. You will give yourself that extra bit of time and the more positively you start your day the better you will feel. In the chapter on healthy living we covered "Refusing the Snooze". It really does work wonders!

Create thinking time - Thinking time is very important and in the fast paced world in which we live in sometimes we don't feel we have time to schedule in thinking. We need to factor this time in however and slow down and reflect occasionally or stop and take stock and amend plans. It is a false perception that you don't have time to stop and think. You need to do this to save time!

Set yourself limits - Setting yourself personal limits is a useful thing to do at work or can be applied to anything else that you tend to do too much of. If you work ten to twelve hour days, for example, set a limit of eight hours per day, and stick to it. Just learn to work smarter and manage your time better and be realistic about what you can achieve in the time scale.

Plan time with family and friends - Plan and literally diarise time for your partner, friends, children or other family members. This may sound a bit regimented, however it will ensure that you don't end up neglecting those who are most important to you. Be very disciplined then not to let people down. So schedule time with them on a regular basis to do something together.

Develop new interests and hobbies - You are never too old to learn something new and there is just so much out there that you could do. It is really important with all the demands that you have in your life that you increase quality time to invest in yourself and your own personal development.

Manage mobile technology - Whilst mobile technology can be very useful it has one of the biggest impacts on our lives simply because it is so intrusive. If you are constantly at the beck and call of your phone then the chances are, even when you think you are spending time with your family, in reality you really are not because you simply are not present with them!

Take holidays - All work and no play. Need I say more? Holidays are the very best way to relax, de stress and recharge. It is really important to take the holidays that you are entitled to.

One other important thing to really consider is the distinction between work and home and to be aware of the negativities that we can potentially carry between the two. If you are not careful, it can become a bad habit that, at the end of each busy day, you offload to our partners all our moans and groans about our work day, thus infecting our home lives with the stress of work. A good habit to get into is to spend time at the end of each day sharing your achievements and successes and focusing on the positive outcomes of the day.

Get everyone to share the three best highlights of their day and focus on the good things that have happened.

Work and home life are equally important, and the key to happiness is about finding the right balance so you can get the best and the most out of both of them.

> *When people go to work, they shouldn't*
> *have to leave their hearts at home*

Betty Bender

Life Balance - Six Steps to Success

1. Schedule brief breaks for yourself throughout the day

2. At the end of each day, set your priorities for the following day

3. Make a distinction between work and the rest of your life

4. Make sure you take all of your allocated holidays

5. Create a buffer between work and home

6. Make time for exercise and relaxation

Positive Thinking

A pessimist sees the difficulty
in every opportunity; an optimist
sees the opportunity in every difficulty

Winston Churchill

This is my favourite life skill and the one that has been, for me personally, the most useful. I believe that positive thinking is the key to happiness and wellbeing. A positive attitude is not about a magical mystical mindset possessed by the lucky few. It is something that everyone is capable of achieving and is simply an inclination or leaning toward the positive aspects of any given situation.

Thinking positively is also not about putting your head in the sand and being unrealistic as some people believe. A positive attitude recognises the negative aspects of a situation, however makes a conscious decision to focus instead on the hope and opportunity that is available. This releases you from getting locked in a paralysing loop of bad feeling and allows you to move quickly to take action and solve difficulties.

Positive thinking and optimism are now known to be a root cause of many life benefits. The relatively new science of *psychoneuroimmunology* looks at how our mind can influence our immune system. The theory is that you will live longer and be healthier and happier by cultivating a positive attitude toward life. In addition, you are more likely to be successful, maintain better relationships and have a beneficial influence on those around you.

Your mental approach to life is a combination of your thoughts, emotions and beliefs. Becoming aware of your emotions, identifying and analysing your thoughts and understanding your beliefs is key to really being able to tackle how you deal with what comes your way.

Be Positive

Avoid negative attitude germs - You may have noticed that when you are with someone who is suffering from a physical or emotional problem, you feel bad too. It's often described as catching their emotion. Researchers have observed this actually happening in real time in the brain, using an advanced MRI (Magnetic Resonance Imaging) machine. It shows the brain of Person A reflects activity in the same area as Person B when they are in close proximity.

The scientific term for this is *neural mirroring*. This does, therefore, point out the danger of hanging around negative, pessimistic people if you prefer to be positive and optimistic. It also means that if you are feeling negative and you dump your negativity on others they can catch your negative attitude germs!

Choose to be a radiator - Some people you meet are like drains: negative, listless doom goblins and when we come into contact with them they drain us of energy.

They like to tell you about all their negative news and prefer to play the victim, wallowing in the "poor me" mentality. These are the people who when you ask them how they are they will respond by giving you a graphic blow by blow account of all their woes and feelings of impending doom! You may well know people like this. Perhaps it is something we are all guilty of from time to time.

Other people, however, are like radiators, full of warmth and vitality. We feel positively energised by them. They appear bright and radiant, look you in the eye and when you ask them how they are, they smile and tell you something positive.

Take personal responsibility - Amazingly enough the antidote for negativity is that you learn to accept responsibility for your situation. The very act of taking responsibility cancels out any negative emotion that you may trigger. By embracing responsibility you will reap many rewards. The successes brought by this attitude act as a foundation for self-respect, pride and confidence.

It can be easy to blame others or circumstances for everything in our lives – past, present or future. It lets us off the hook to some degree. However, ultimately it doesn't help us because we become a prisoner of circumstance and allow everything and everyone around us to dictate our world.

Positively learn from mistakes - Making mistakes is human and we can't get everything right all the time. To increase your rate of success you will have to be willing to accept that you will make mistakes along the way, the skill is that you positively learn from them. Certainly some of the best learning and character building experiences I have been through are on the back of mistakes.

Recognising and admitting that you made a mistake and addressing what you can to improve the situation can be very liberating.

For example admitting when we get something wrong and saying I'm sorry can relieve a great deal of tension in any relationship. Humble pie can actually taste quite nice! It isn't poisonous. It is a real skill to be brave enough to admit when you don't get something right and have the humility to accept it, admit it and then positively move on.

Eliminate excuses - You can create your own self limitations if you focus on all the reasons why you can't do something. If you search hard enough you will find loads of excuses I am sure. It is really important that you challenge this way of thinking because you will totally limit your potential. You will miss out on so many possibilities and exciting opportunities. Sometimes we make excuses because we are afraid of failing or we fear the unknown, or maybe it is because we are too lazy to give it a go! Challenge yourself next time you make an excuse and really examine the reason behind it!

Life can be an interesting and challenging journey and granted you may well be faced with some pretty challenging situations.

However, by developing a positive attitude you will be much better equipped to be able to deal with everything so much better. It takes practice and certainly there will be days when you really struggle to see the bright side. The light at the end of the tunnel may well feel beyond reach. You may even decide you want to wallow a little and feel a bit sorry for yourself and that is ok. The question though, is for how long?

Eventually you need to turn it around and seek out the opportunity that can arise from any problematic situation .The word *probortunity* is a hybrid of the words problem and opportunity. Using the word probortunity instead of problem is a good way of addressing anything that is challenging in a positive and optimistic way .

A firm belief that everything has the potential for a positive outcome is helpful. Even when things don't turn out exactly as we would like them too, at the very least, the positive is that we will have learnt from the experience. Even when we experience pain it will make us appreciate the pleasurable times even more!

> *Become a possibilitarian. No matter how dark things seem to be or actually are, raise your sights and see possibilities - always see them, for they're always there*

Norman Vincent Peale

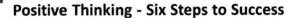

Positive Thinking - Six Steps to Success

1. Make the decision to be a more positive person

2. Become very aware of your thinking and internal voice

3. Use positive internal language to condition your thinking

4. Challenge any excuses you make to yourself

5. Be a radiator and manage your negative attitude germs

6. Seek out opportunities through problematic situations

Problem Solving

Problems are to the mind what exercise is to the muscles, they toughen and make strong

Norman Vincent Peale

Developing a positive attitude toward problems can transform you into a happier and more confident person who will feel so much more in control of your life. You can learn to respond to problems with enthusiasm and eagerness, rising to the challenge to show your stuff and actually amaze yourself with some of the results you can achieve! It is very much about how you view each situation.

I read something once that suggested that problems were opportunities with thorns on which I thought was a rather good description. Let's face it we don't exactly wake up in the morning hoping that we will experience problems, however it is pretty inevitable that we will from time to time.

We covered in the previous chapter on positive thinking the concept of creating the hybrid word probortunity from problem and opportunity. This is a great way to approach each challenge and will help you to cultivate a more positive perspective.

Problems really can be seen as an opportunity which could well provide you with a chance to get out of a rut you have been in for a while or a chance to make a situation better. Problems need not be as a result of external factors or bad events. Any new awareness you have that allows you to see possibilities for improvement brings along with it a problem for you to solve. This is why the most creative people seek out problems rather than avoid them.

How you view problem solving is simply a matter of choice. You can view each problem as a giant rock in the road that is an insurmountable obstacle if you want to. Or you can work out ways and create your own strategy of how you can navigate your way around it.

Problem solving is an important life skill because it is also a very useful tool to help you tackle immediate challenges or achieve a goal. It is a skill because once you have learnt it you can use it repeatedly.

There are a variety of problem solving processes, however each process consists of a series of steps, including identifying an issue, searching for options and putting a possible solution into action. It is useful to view problem solving as a cycle because, sometimes, a problem needs several attempts to solve it, or the problem changes.

Here is a process that I recommend and will help you to break the problem into easier stages rather than tackle everything all at once.

How To Solve Problems

⇨ Identify the problem and focus on solving one aspect at a time

⇨ Define exactly what the problem is in the clearest and most simple terms

⇨ Conduct a root cause analysis working out exactly what the source of the problem is

⇨ Generate a range of potential solutions and make a short list

⇨ Use the goal that you are trying to achieve to help you to select the solution

⇨ Prepare a plan of action and implement the solution

⇨ Review, identify lessons learnt and record for future reference

Identifying and naming the problem will help you find an appropriate solution. Sometimes you might be unsure about what the problem is and you might just feel general anxiety or be confused about what is getting in the way of your goals. When you know exactly what you are dealing with you will feel more in control and actually less afraid. It is also important to have an understanding of what caused the problem. This will help you to put it into perspective and give it some context.

When you are clear about what the problem is you need to think about it in different ways. Seeing the problem in different ways is likely to help you to find an effective solution. This is where creativity can be really helpful, so that you can explore all options available to you.

From the list of possible solutions, you can sort out which are most relevant to your situation and which are realistic and manageable. You can do this by predicting outcomes for possible solutions and being clear about the goal that you are trying to achieve. Your goal will ultimately be used to benchmark the success of your chosen solution.

It is also useful to check with other people what they think of your plan and invite feedback. When you have explored all the consequences, you can use this information to identify the solution which is most relevant and is likely to have the best outcome.

Implementing your solution will be easier because you will have so much more confidence knowing that you have really thought it through.

You can prepare yourself to implement the solution by planning when and how you will do it and who you will need to communicate with for support and co-operation.

Remember, just because you have worked your way through the problem solving process, it does not mean that that you automatically solve your problem. It is advisable to have an alternative back up plan.

Problem solving is a skill and applying a process which you can learn and practice will not only improve your ability. It is really important to review how you did and make a record of what worked and what didn't so that you can learn and improve your problem solving skills

The more you actively and positively embrace some of the challenges that you will inevitably have to deal with in life, the better equipped and more confident you will become. This will provide you with the opportunity to gather a whole raft of experience that will help you to solve future problems. You will also be able to help other people by sharing some of your experiences.

> *If you only have a hammer, you tend to see every problem as a nail*

Abraham Maslow

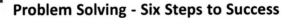

Problem Solving - Six Steps to Success

1. Be positive and view your problems as opportunities

2. Specifically identify and understand each problem

3. Be creative and explore a range of options

4. Determine your goal to help you select your solution

5. Prepare a plan to implement your solution

6. Analyse and review your problem solving approach

Relationship Building

*The most important ingredient
we put into any relationship
is not what we say or
what we do, but what we are*

Stephen R. Covey

When you cultivate positive and supportive relationships in your life you are more likely to feel happier and more fulfilled. When relationships work well, it can be a very happy experience. However, as I am sure you may well have experienced, when relationships break down and you find yourself in a conflict situation, it can be draining and disappointing and have a detrimental effect on your wellbeing.

Before you begin to develop positive relationships with others you need to make sure that you have a healthy relationship with yourself. In the chapter later on which looks at self confidence we will explore this concept in more detail because it is a key consideration.

One of the biggest challenges we experience in relationships is that we are all different and we can perceive the world in so many different ways. Certainly a stumbling block that we come across when we try to build relationships is a desire or an expectation of the way that people will think and behave.

The first step however, to building successful relationships is to accept that we are all different and on that basis can bring different things to the party. You will have your own unique set of strengths and as a result you will have your own unique set of limitations. It is indeed better and more productive to spend time concentrating on improving your own limitations rather than focusing on those of others.

In the chapter on communication we looked at different personality styles and this is a good basis for beginning to understand strengths and limitations.

Focusing on other people's better qualities and feeding back about their strengths is a way to reinforce future positive behaviour. Many relationships break down because more time is spent eroding each other's self-esteem through negative criticism. The danger is that we can try to get other people to shrink fit into something or somebody that they are not. Also, it is important to recognise that often, what we don't like in others can be something that we don't like in ourselves!

There are a few key behaviours that will help you to develop positive relationships and I have outlined here some tips and advice that you can take on board to improve your interpersonal skills.

Building Positive Relationships

Listen - Listening is a hugely important skill in terms of boosting another person's self-esteem. It is the silent form of flattery that makes people feel supported and valued. Listening and understanding what others communicate to us is the most important part of successful interaction and vice versa. When a person decides to communicate with another person, they do so to fulfil a need. We were given two ears and one mouth, because for some people listening is twice as hard as talking!.

Be Present - Being present with people is very important, so that, when you are with someone, you are truly with them in that moment and not dwelling on something else. The connection we make with other people is the very touchstone of our existence and devoting time, energy and effort into developing and building relationships is one of the most valuable life skills. This is why giving yourself total permission to fully focus on the person when you are with them is essential.

Give and take feedback - From your own personal perspective any feedback that you receive is free information and you have the choice entirely whether you want to take it on board or not.

It is a great service with regards to helping you to tap into your blind spot and very useful in terms of helping you to get a different perspective. Remember, it is the food of progress!

Trust more - To trust someone takes courage. However, no matter what our own personal baggage, is the more we trust people the more we can learn. The first step to developing trust is to learn to trust ourselves. Trusting ourselves to be able to cope when someone we care about hurts us. Trusting ourselves to do the best we are capable of doing for most of the time. Trusting ourselves to never give up hope that tomorrow will be brighter and that even if it's not we will handle it. Once you have mastered this you will be more open and receptive to trust others and understand that even if someone lets us down it's because we are all human and not infallible.

Manage your mobile - By now, pretty much everyone has a mobile phone and quite a few people I know have two - one for work and one for personal use. While mobile phones are a lifesaver in an emergency, and an effective tool for communication, they can also be a complete distraction when people exhibit a lack of mobile phone etiquette. We have covered a little bit about this already in the chapter on communication. So being self aware of the way that you use your technological appendages is very important! There is a guide at the back of the book on mobile technology etiquette.

Building positive relationships with people is so important for our own sense of wellbeing. We are sociable creatures and connecting with others will help us to feel better about ourselves and life in general.

In a world that has cultivated so many isolated environments and working conditions it is important to examine how much time you spend with people. This also means being in the company of people, not with virtual strangers via the internet and facebook or various other social media networks.

> *The most important single ingredient in the formula of success is knowing how to get along with people*

Theodore Roosevelt

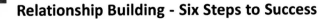

Relationship Building - Six Steps to Success

1. The relationship you have with yourself is the most important

2. Actively listen to what other people have to say

3. Accept and celebrate that everyone is different

4. Focus on people's strengths rather than limitations

5. Be open-minded and learn to trust people

6. Develop etiquette around mobile technology

Relaxation

Tension is who you think you should be.
Relaxation is who you are

Chinese Proverb

Modern living seems to be so much about rushing around, attempting to keep lots of balls in the air and not having time to recover! Building relaxation time into your life is so important. It can help to keep your stress levels down, and consequently maintain and improve your health. Too much work and not enough time out for yourself can result in physical and mental health problems. Taking at least twenty minutes a day to wind down can be enough. Whether it's soaking in a lovely warm bubble bath or doing a quick relaxation session before going to sleep or simply listening to some relaxing music.

There are so many wonderful ways that you can relax. Relaxation is the key when it comes to stress relief therapies. Studies have shown evidence of many other benefits coming from regular relaxation treatments. These may include a decrease in the risk of heart attack, protection from mental health issues, a boost for your immune system and even an improvement for your memory.

Stress levels are so much higher than they used to be and it is important for your health to bring these levels down. Finding time for yourself may be difficult, however, it is essential for your wellbeing that you keep anxiety at bay. If your levels of stress hormones are raised they can cause your blood pressure to rise, making your brain behave differently.

If you are challenged with sleepless nights you will know how it feels to have your mind buzzing with anxiety while you are desperately in need sleep. Relaxation can help you switch off and promote much better quality of sleep which in turn will help you to recharge your batteries and cope better generally.

Some people do find it challenging to relax and very often I will hear people say that they simply don't have enough time. It can be challenging to find time, especially if you're a generally busy person, however to avoid burn-out it is essential to plan in time for relaxation.

One simple method that is easy to build in to the fabric of your day is a warm bath. Warm water and a bubble bath will loosen up your muscles and it's a great way to feel pampered without really doing a lot. It will also deepen respiration and take any tension away from your body which will push all the stresses and strains of the day straight down the plughole! Fifteen minutes soaking in a warm bubble bath will help you feel relaxed and lighten your mind. Candles and calming music can be an additional way to luxuriate.

Music is also a great way of helping you to relax, relieve stress and any anxieties you may have. It also helps you function mentally and physically, which is why music is a great therapy. It's regularly used for meditation and as an aid for sleep disorders. Studies have suggested that slow, gentle, soothing music can improve learning, creativity and memory. I recommend *Pachelbel's Canon in D minor*. It is wonderful!

Breathing has to be the easiest form of relaxation and when you focus on breathing it can really help you to calm down if you are feeling stressed. There are many simple breathing exercises that are simple and require no equipment and can be done anywhere.

Relaxation Breathing

⇨ Sit with your back straight

⇨ Place the tip of your tongue behind your upper front teeth

⇨ Close your mouth and inhale quietly through your nose to a mental count of four.

⇨ Hold your breath for a count of four.

⇨ Exhale completely through your mouth, slowly, to a count of eight.

This is one breath. Now repeat this six times. This simple and effective breathing method will help you to relax.

Another useful relaxation technique is something called "Mindfulness". The term comes from Eastern spiritual and religious traditions like Zen Buddhism. Mental health professionals are beginning to recognise that mindfulness can have many benefits for people suffering from difficulties such as anxiety and depression. A growing number of scientific studies are showing the benefits of mindfulness in many aspects of our lives including our physical and mental well-being, our relationships and our performance at school and at work.

Mindfulness refers to being completely in touch with and aware of the present moment, as well as taking a non-evaluative and non-judgmental approach to your inner experience. It is essentially about being present and noticing what is around you. So often we can find it hard to relax and be in the moment because we are so preoccupied with the past or worrying about something that hasn't even happened yet.

By focusing on the moment and enjoying the experience rather than being somewhere else will heighten your enjoyment of whatever activity you are involved in. Tapping into and focusing on all your senses will help you to appreciate much more what is going on around you which in turn can have a very relaxing effect.

There are also some very good remedies that can work well to help you to unwind. Herbal teas are good, especially camomile and lavender drops on your pillow at night can be effective to promote sleep. If you visit your local health store you can be sure that you will discover a whole host of remedies.

The benefits of building relaxation into your day are multiple and chilling out is a way to not only look after yourself physically, mentally and emotionally, it is also the best way to soothe the soul.

> *Take rest; a field that has rested gives a bountiful crop*

Ovid

Relaxation - Six Steps to Success

1. Build in time every day for relaxation

2. Identify different relaxation methods that work for you

3. Listen to music to help you relax

4. Use simple breathing techniques to de-stress

5. Explore the range of relaxation remedies

6. Learn to be mindful and enjoy the moment

Resilience

*Our greatest glory is not in never falling,
but in rising every time we fall*

Confucius

It is inevitable that you will experience adversity and setbacks throughout your lifetime. Sometimes we simply cannot change circumstances however we do have total choice in terms of how we react to them.

The ability to bounce back and recover is a quality that is well worth investing in and will help to equip you to be able to deal with the demands and challenges of everyday living. You may have heard the expression "what doesn't kill you makes you stronger" and you may well have experienced that in your own life. Clearly, some people have the ability to spring back from difficulties and trauma more successfully than others.

Resilience comes from the Latin word "resilio" which means "to jump back" and is used in everyday language to describe our ability to cope with and bounce back from adversity. Some people describe it as the ability to bend instead of breaking when under pressure or difficulty or the ability to persevere and adapt when faced with challenges. The same abilities also help to make us more open to and willing to take on new opportunities. In this way being resilient is more than just survival, it is also about letting go and learning to grow.

A resilient person is not only able to handle difficult experiences as they happen, they are also good at bouncing back quickly afterwards. The good news is that we can all develop our resilience by managing our thoughts, behaviours and actions.

Personal Resilience

Take emotional control - Some people internalise and withdraw when something difficult and challenging happens. Some people like to externalise and let the whole world know about it. Some people can be total drama queens and turn molehills in mountains. Being emotionally aware and cultivating your ability to recognise how you can potentially react in certain situations will help you to take more self control. It will also help you to be more considerate with regards to how your reaction can affect other people.

Avoid being a victim - There is a huge risk, when something difficult arises, for us to feel sorry for ourselves, It isn't very helpful and very often will drive us further away from where we really want to be. Some people however seem to derive some sort of comfort from playing the victim and asking the questions "Why does this always happen to me?". It strikes me however, that people who choose to adopt this attitude have some kind of expectation that someone else will come along and "fix" their problem. Not only is this kind of mentality self centred it is also very draining on other people.

Take responsibility - By taking responsibility for our circumstances and not looking for ways to apportion blame it will enable you to seek out solutions. That is by the far the most progressive and productive way to approach any adversity. We are so much more in control than we think sometimes and if you find yourself sitting in the passenger seat then you need to get in to driving seat and navigate your own way through whatever it is you are experiencing.

Be optimistic - Optimism is about being hopeful and believing that this time will pass and there is the potential for things to improve. Realistic optimism is important, not pie-in-the-sky optimism. People who are blindly optimistic who, for example, stick their heads in the sand, do not have the brand of optimism which facilitates problem solving, in fact it can interfere with it.

Staying positive during dark periods can be difficult, but maintaining a hopeful outlook is important. Being an optimist does not mean ignoring the problem in order to focus on positive outcomes. It means understanding that setbacks are transient and that you have the skills and abilities to combat the challenges you face.

Be flexible - Flexibility is an essential part of resilience. By learning how to be more adaptable, you will be much better equipped to respond to adversity or any life crisis you experience. Resilient people often utilize these events as an opportunity to branch out in new directions. While some people may be crushed by abrupt changes, highly resilient individuals are able to adapt and thrive. When we accept that there is no such thing as forever and that everything changes we start to bend not break.

Look after yourself - When you're stressed, it can be all too easy to neglect your own needs. Losing your appetite, overeating, not exercising, not getting enough sleep, drinking too much alcohol, not drinking enough water, driving yourself too hard, are all common reactions to a crisis situation. Focus on building your self-nurturance skills, especially when you are troubled. Make time to relax and to embark in activities that you know make you feel better. Take time to invest into your well being and you will boost your overall health and resilience and be fully ready to face life's challenges. Remember, at times like this you are more vulnerable and prone to illness so make sure you indulge in a little tender loving care.

SUMO - A key part of resilience is the ability to let go. Some people are intent on carrying so much personal baggage around with them which makes it difficult to move on. There is a great book by Paul McCann called SUMO which means to shut up and move on. We cannot change the past. The best we can do is learn from it and move on!

There really are some wonderful examples of how people react to some quite extreme situations that are both heart-warming and encouraging. Human beings most certainly are quite extraordinary creatures and, on occasions, we can surprise ourselves with the strength and potential we possess. If we believe that we have the capacity to be able to deal with even the most extreme situation we can not only develop our own internal resources and confidence; we can also be an inspiration and provide hope for others.

He's a million rubber bands in his resilience
- Alan K. Simpson

Confucius

Resilience - Six Steps to Success

1. Take emotional control

2. Avoid adopting a victim mentality

3. Be optimistic and keep an open, flexible mind

4. Believe in your ability to overcome adversity

5. SUMO - Shut up and move on

6. Learn and grow from every experience

Self Confidence

A man cannot be comfortable
without his own approval

Mark Twain

The real key to self-confidence is about believing in yourself and trusting your own views and opinions. At times, this can be difficult, especially if you have a tendency to listen to others and benchmark yourself against what they think of you. This can leave you very vulnerable and the ability to establish your own inner benchmark to success is essential.

Every human being has the ability to take control and make positive changes. Other people may try and stop you, but only if you allow them. When you look in the mirror, be proud of the person that you see, knowing that you do the best that you can.

The most important relationship that you will ever have is the relationship you have with yourself. Would you choose to be your best friend? If you don't like yourself or believe in yourself then how do you expect anyone else to? You need to like and enjoy the person who you are. Embrace your strengths and accept your imperfections of which everyone has some. It would be very dull being perfect. Being a person in progress will give you something to work on, something to aspire to!

Working on your own self-confidence is a very good investment of time and energy. There is a fine line between arrogance and confidence, and it is important to be honest with yourself as well as seeking feedback from others to gain a balanced perspective. It is also important, however, that you don't rely on others to big you up and make you feel better. It is important that you learn how to recognise and appreciate yourself when you have done something well. If you rely on others all the time or become so preoccupied with other people's opinions of you, it can create insecurity and paranoia. It is about establishing a balanced view point.

Imagine having no-one to compare yourself with except yourself. What a sense of relief this would bring. We wouldn't have to worry about not looking like the alpha male or female with the smartest mind, the most important job role and the biggest pay packet. We wouldn't have to worry about our bodies not being the youngest, most beautiful and most sexy.

All you would have to think is: did I do this activity better than I did it last week? Have I moved forward in my own definition of success? Am I doing my best for my health? Do I have an attractive mind and healthy relationships with other people?

Here are few key actions that you need to take on board to build your self confidence.

Building Confidence

Take personal responsibility - Take a good look at yourself in the metaphorical mirror and start by being really honest. What is your true opinion of yourself? Are you appreciative of all your strengths and qualities? Or do you beat yourself up on a regular basis about all your misgivings, mistakes and weaknesses? We have to take responsibility for being the best that we can be. So often we will compare ourselves to others, and if we do this, we run the danger of engendering two emotions, one of vanity or one of bitterness, because there will always be people we see as better or worse off than ourselves. It is also pointless to benchmark ourselves against others. Using yourself as your own benchmark is far more constructive.

Build self awareness - Self-awareness is a recognition of our personality, your strengths and weaknesses, your likes and dislikes. Knowing and understanding who you are and what makes you tick is essential if you want to tap into your potential. Developing self-awareness can help you to recognise when you are stressed or under pressure. Self-awareness is the first step in the creation process. As you grow in self-awareness, you will understand yourself better and know why you feel what you do and why you behave as you behave. That understanding then gives you the opportunity and freedom to change those things you would like to change about yourself and create the life you want. Without fully knowing who you are, self-acceptance and change is impossible.

Be the best you can be - When you think negatively about yourself, you may well project that feeling on to others in the form of insults and gossip. To break this cycle of negativity, get into the habit of praising other people. Refuse to engage in backstabbing gossip and make an effort to compliment those around you instead. In the process, you'll become well-liked and, by looking for the best in others, you will, indirectly, bring out the best in yourself.

Use positive language - It's time to have a little chat with yourself and really listen to your personal vocabulary. How do you talk to yourself? Vocabulary is something we very rarely pay conscious attention to, yet it can give away a whole host of information about us to the perceptive listener. Your appearance, vocabulary and speech form part of the all important "first impression" you make on other people. While the tone and timbre of our voices creates either a pleasing or grating effect on the listener, our choice of words conveys our attitude and emotional stance. There is a very interesting relationship between vocabulary and attitude.

Challenge your beliefs - One of the biggest inhibitors to cultivating self confidence is the limiting beliefs that we can carry around with us. Sometimes we may not even be aware of the excuses that we make which can stop us from tapping in to our potential. Fear of failure is one of the biggest obstacles. It is so important to listen to your internal dialogue and challenge anything that stops you from being the very best that you can be.

> *Make the most of yourself, for that is all there is of you*

Ralph Waldo Emerson

Self Confidence - Six Steps to Success

1. Be your own best friend
2. Take personal responsibility
3. Be self aware and understand yourself
4. Be the best that you can be
5. Use positive language
6. Challenge your beliefs

Stress Management

*Adopting the right attitude can convert
a negative stress into a positive one*

Hans Selye

I think it would be fair to say that a little bit of pressure can be positive. It can, if it is managed successfully, galvanise and help you to perform better at something. However, too much pressure or prolonged pressure can lead to stress, which is unhealthy for the mind and body. Everyone reacts differently to stress, and some people may have a higher threshold than others. Too much stress can often lead to physical, mental and emotional problems.

Stress is your body's way of responding to any kind of demand or pressure. It can be caused by both positive and negative experiences. When faced with a situation that makes you stressed, your body releases chemicals, including cortisol, adrenaline and noradrenalin.

These chemicals give people more energy and strength, which can be a good thing if their stress is caused by physical danger. This, however, can also be a bad thing, if their stress is in response to something emotional and there is no outlet for this extra energy and strength.

Many different things can cause stress. Identifying what may be causing them is the first step in learning how to cope. Some of the most common sources of stress are:

Survival Stress - You may have heard the phrase "fight or flight"; this is a common response to danger in all people and animals. When you are afraid that someone or something may be trying to hurt you, your body naturally responds with a burst of energy so that you will be better able to survive the dangerous situation (fight) or escape it altogether (flight).

Internal stress - Have you ever worried about things that have happened that you can do nothing about and that you have absolutely no control over? We all do, I am sure, from time to time. This is internal stress and it is one of the most important kinds of stress to understand and manage. Internal stress is when people make themselves stressed and anxious.

Stress releases certain chemicals into your system that can be highly addictive and some people become "stress junkies" by getting off on a chemical high. They may even look for stressful situations and feel stressed about things that aren't stressful. This, for some people, like coffee, is a stimulant that acts as false energy and motivation.

Environmental stress - This is a response to things around you that cause stress, such as noise, crowding and pressure from work or family. Identifying these environmental stresses and learning to avoid them or deal with them will help lower your stress level. Certainly some people are more sensitive to this than others and find it more difficult to filter out environmental distractions.

Workplace stress - This kind of stress builds up over a long time and can take a hard toll on your body. It can be caused by working too much or too hard and not getting your work – home balance into a healthy perspective. It can also be caused by not knowing how to manage your time well or knowing how to take time out for rest and relaxation. This can be one of the hardest kinds of stress to avoid because many people feel this is out of their control.

Stress can affect both your body and your mind. People under large amounts of stress can become tired, sick, and unable to concentrate or think clearly. Sometimes, stress can even trigger severe depression and mental breakdowns.

Managing Stress

Here are a few suggestions of things that that you can do to cope with stress:

Control your thoughts - One of the best ways to tackle stress is to address your thinking. When the subconscious mind is told something by the conscious mind it doesn't distinguish between what is real and what is artificial. It will believe whatever you tell it. Therefore, if you tell yourself that you are stressed, then you will be. The danger is sometimes stress can become a habit and you may attach a way of thinking to a certain set of circumstances. For example if you were stressed in a certain situation last time you talk yourself into believing that you will be again so then it become a self fulfilling prophecy.

Be more assertive - Assertiveness is a great communication skill to develop, especially when we simply do not have enough time on our hands and we have to say no to a request. Also, if you are a passive or aggressive communicator poor communication skills can add to your stress levels.

Manage your time - A great deal of stress is associated with the perceived time restraints that we have. The feeling that we simply don't have enough time to do everything we need to do is common for many people. We are just about to cover time management in the next chapter so you will learn more about how to do this.

Avoid caffeine - Research has indicated that caffeine increases the secretion of stress hormones like adrenaline, so if you are already secreting higher stress hormones, caffeine will boost it even higher and exacerbate stress/anxiety or depression even further than it already is. By cutting caffeine you will lower your stress hormone levels and therefore reduce stress, anxiety and depression.

Exercise more - The benefits of exercise are numerous, as I hope I have already expressed in the previous chapter. Not only does it release a chemical called serotonin, which makes you feel happier and less stressed, it also improves circulation and helps prevent conditions such as stroke and heart attack. Exercise also allows you to take out your frustration and anger in a constructive way through a very positive channel.

Learn to let go - Learning to let go of the past or things that you fear may happen in the future is a big help when managing stress. We cannot change the past and we cannot control the future. What we can do is deal with the here and now, slow down and go with the flow.

> *There is more to life than increasing its speed*

Gandhi

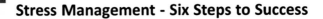

Stress Management - Six Steps to Success

1. Control your thoughts to manage your stress levels

2. Learn to be more confident and assertive

3. Manage your time efficiently

4. Use exercise to alleviate stress

5. Reduce caffeine and alcohol

6. Learn to let go and go with the flow

Time Management

But what minutes! Count them by sensation,
and not by calendars, and each moment is a day

Benjamin Disraeli

Imagine if time was a bank account and, each morning, you were credited with 86,400 seconds. If, by the end of that day you hadn't spent any of the credits they would instantly be deducted from your account. What would you do?

Well the chances are, I expect, that you would make every effort to spend them. It's amazing, isn't it, how much we take time for granted and then regret the moments we lose or waste?

In transport economics, the value of time is the opportunity cost of the time that a traveller spends on their journey. In essence, this makes it the amount that a traveller would be willing to pay in order to save time, or the amount they would accept as compensation for lost time. The value of time varies considerably from person to person and depends upon the purpose of the journey, but can generally be divided into two sets of valuations: working time and non-working time. I guess that sums up life very well and as we have already covered life balance it is important that we make a balanced investment into both work and play time.

One of the biggest challenges that many people face is personal time management and the ability to prioritise. Let's face it, we all have our own quirky little habits that we have adopted and I am sure we have all been guilty of putting ourselves and other people under unnecessary pressure by just not being as well-organised as we could be. This can have a big effect on our stress levels too .The more efficiently we manage our time, the better we will feel generally.

It is also important to respect other people's time and, if our own lack of personal organisation or timekeeping disrupts others, then it is important that we take responsibility and do something about it.

Also, it is worth considering that, no matter how organised we may be, there are always only 24 hours in a day. Time doesn't change. All we can actually manage is ourselves and what we do with the time that we have. Many of us are prey to time-wasters who steal time that we could be using much more productively. It is so easy to go off-track or become distracted by something that is so much more interesting than the task in hand.

Procrastination is the ultimate thief of time, and putting off what we can do today is something many people are guilty of. It is actually far better to do the thing you least like doing first so that it doesn't hang over you making you feel gloomy at the prospect.

It is important to remember, the focus of time management is actually changing your behaviours, not changing time. So here are a few tips of how you can do that:

Managing Time

Review Time - Have you ever stopped and really analysed how you spend your time ? It is a really useful exercise for 14 days to record how you spend your 86,400 seconds so keep a log and this will be a good place to start changing any unhelpful habits.

Eliminating your personal time-wasters - Once you know how you are spending your time you will easily begin to see how you waste time. Very often it will be things that you can change and being honest with yourself will help.

Create a system - It's amazing how so many people don't have a good system in place and work rather randomly and react to whatever comes along. It is a far better approach to be proactive and have more control over your day. Making a priority plan will help you to stay focused. Learning how to manage emails can be helpful. One system I use is that when I have an email in my inbox I make a decision straight away of what to do with it rather than open it and go back to it later. I either action it, delete it or file it.

Avoid procrastination - It is so tempting to put off what you don't like doing to another time or even another day or week. One of the best pieces advice that I have had is to do what you least like doing first. Get it over and done with and I guarantee you will feel lighter and more motivated .There is nothing worse than having something hanging over you. It slows you down and makes you feel heavy.

Avoid the "Superhero Syndrome" - Some people are their own worst enemy because they want to portray the image of someone who is infallible and capable of taking the world on their shoulders as a cartoon superhero might! We are not however superheroes we are human, therefore we are not infallible and there really is only so much that you can do. Learning to negotiate and on occasions even saying no is not only necessary it is essential and will take the pressure away, and you are less likely to let people down and stress yourself out!

Be Tidy - The tidier and the more minimalistic you are the easier it will be to find things and this can save lots of time. It is also good for your mind because it will help you to focus and feel more in control. Other people you work around will also appreciate you being tidy as it makes life better and easier for them too.

> *A man who dares to waste one hour*
> *of life has not discovered the value of life*

Charles Darwin

Time Management - Six Steps to Success

1. Value your time and other people's

2. Review where you are spending your time

3. Create time management systems

4. Avoid procrastinating and get things done

5. Be tidy and put things away

6. Plan tomorrow today

Value and Purpose

It is our choices that show what we truly are,
far more than our abilities

J.K. Rowling

For some people, adding value and having a purpose in life is an essential and fundamental aim. For others, fulfilment and purpose is halted by fear of failure or lack of motivation or just a blind desire to want to pleasure seek for themselves only .

A great deal of research now suggests that people who have meaning and purpose in their lives are happier, feel more in control and get more out of everything they do. They also experience less stress, less anxiety and are less prone to experience prolonged bouts of depression.

Something that we all need to do rather than racing around like headless chickens wondering what it's all about is to stop and explore our purpose.

It helps us to answer the burning questions of "Why are we here?" and "What's it all about anyway?" Often it's something that can't be distilled into one definitive thing and goes far beyond the day-to-day activity. It guides us in how we choose to live our lives, what we strive for and provides a framework and measurement for the goals that we set ourselves. It can help us to make sense of what happens to us. It can provide a source of comfort and strength in challenging and difficult periods of our lives and most of all helps us feel that we are not alone, because we are part of something much bigger.

Personally, I like the concept that we are all connected and that if we hurt others, we will only end up hurting ourselves, so we have a purpose to be kind and considerate in our behaviour towards others. By taking more personal responsibility for the consequences of our actions, our purpose becomes more honourable. If we approach every life situation with positive and kind intentions, then we will be making our own great individual contribution to creating a better world.

For some people finding meaning comes through experiences, often difficult ones. Other people find their meaning through deep reflection, others from loving and being loved and others just from the way they choose to approach other people and the world around. We can each find our own way - but it's important to remember the importance of meaning when making the big choices about our families, jobs, lifestyles and priorities.

Some people see their meaning as finding their 'calling'. What is certain is that 'meaning' is something very personal. No one else can tell us what gives meaning to our lives and if we rely on others rather than taking personal responsibility we leave ourselves vulnerable. We have to discover different ways of finding meaning. We need to explore and indentify and pursue our own purpose with a positive intention of making the world a better place.

Make a difference

Lead the way - A good example has twice the value of good advice. When we endeavor to do things to make a difference, we should also seek to influence others to start doing things that make a difference too. The best way to convince other people is to lead by example. Start doing whatever is within your ability today. Start showing more consideration for the people you live with, work with and come into contact with each day. Every effort counts, no matter how small and insignificant it may seem. Just do something, and do something good.

Respect and value others - I am sure that you have witnessed someone getting treated unfairly. It happens both professionally and socially, sometimes individuals who deserve recognition do not get it. Perhaps they are scared of confrontation and find it hard to stand up for themselves. By taking up the fight and making sure others get what they deserve and earned you will make a lasting impact on their lives. They in turn will get the justice they deserve and feel better. Be careful that you get all the information right though before you go jumping in feet first.

Random acts of kindness - There are so many that you can do. It's the little things that can make another persons' day, like helping someone with a heavy case or a pram, holding open a door, picking up some litter. It really doesn't need to be huge. Having the courage to compliment someone if they look nice is lovely and can make someone glow all day. You have most likely been on the receiving end of some kind act so I am sure you know how good it makes you feel.

Develop an attitude of gratitude - Making a conscious decision to be grateful for who you are and what you have in your life is a very positive way to behave. This will also help you to value everything that you have in your life and not take anything for granted. Research suggests that if you practice gratitude on a daily basis after 28 days you can increase your happiness levels by 25%.

Be happy - Happiness and love are two of the greatest gifts you can give to the world. Too often, we can be so absorbed in our own little bubble and we forget that there are people in this world who we can make a little happier and who we can make feel a little more loved.

You can make a difference right now to yourself and the world around you and be happier. If you know that you are doing the best you can every day in every way then you will know that you add value, and your purpose in life will be to know that you can make a positive difference in everything that you do.

> *You were born an original. Don't die a copy*

John Mason

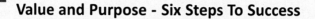

Value and Purpose - Six Steps To Success

1. Identify your purpose and meaning in life
2. Be the change you want the world to be
3. Practise kindness on a daily basis
4. Develop an attitude of gratitude
5. Respect and value other people
6. Be happy and be the best you can be

Mobile Manners

For many people it would be difficult to imagine a life without a mobile phone, or for some, even two or three. It is the most common artificial appendage and whilst there are a multitude of obvious benefits there is also the need for people to observe mobile manners!

These days mobile phone capabilities seem endless. Whilst making calls is the primary function, now you can surf the internet, take photos, record videos, download an entire libraries of information and navigate your way around the world with Google Earth!. With apps galore we are just waiting for the next amazing function.

Mobile phones can also however cause accidents, be a source of immense irritation and have a detrimental effect on interpersonal communication. So often now if a mobile phone bleats it's owner will bow to its beck and call. How many times when you are with someone do you feel marginalized by their technological gadgets?. You may, if you are really lucky get a "Oh sorry do you mind if I just take this call?" More often than not your sentence will be left in midair as something more interesting for your companion comes along!

Wouldn't it be great if every mobile phone came along with a little book of mobile manners that everyone adhered to!

Well here is a list of tips that will help you to manage your mobile and set the example for others to embrace too:

Tip One - Do make the person you are with feel more important than your mobile phone. Be present when you are with people. Switch your phone to silent, or better still, off, and put it away.

Tip Two - Be mindful about not developing a dependency on constant communication. It simply is not healthy. Do you really need to have your phone with you all the time?

Tip Three - Take off your earpiece when you are not on the phone. This will stop you from looking like an extra on Star Trek!. Plus, who wants to talk to someone who is so obviously on call alert.

Tip Four - You don't need to speak louder into your mobile than any other phone you use. These gadgets have incredibly sensitive microphones. Honestly!

Tip Five - Answer your phone as soon as it goes off. Not everyone wants to listen to a mobile phone ringing for ages, even if your latest ring tone sounds 'cool' to you.

Tip Six - Be aware that people around you are listening if you answer your phone in public. Not everyone wants to hear what you are saying to someone else and could find it offensive, embarrassing or just plain boring!

Tip Seven - Absolutely under no circumstances use your mobile phone when you are driving. Let's face it some people have a problems mastering vehicles and phones individually let alone trying to multitask the two together!.This is a recipe for disaster.

Tip Eight - The ultimate display of etiquette has to be not using your mobile phone on the loo. Need I say more ....!

> *Apparently we love our own mobile phones*
> *but we hate everyone else's*

Joe Bob Bridges

Recommended Reading List

There are so many excellent books that can help you to develop your life skills. Here are some of the books have I have read and found extremely useful and inspiring:

Visit my website www.liggywebb.com for more information

Motivate to Win by Richard Denny

Communicate to Win by Richard Denny

Six Thinking Hats by Edward de Bono

Assertiveness and Diversity by Anni Townend

The Extraordinary Reader by Clive Lewis and Anthony Landale

Meditation - The stress solution by Mary Pearson

The Happiness Purpose by Edward De Bono

Succeed for Yourself by Richard Denny

Wellbeing by Cary Cooper and Ivan Robertson

Learning to Think Strategically by Julia Stone

Mind Power by James Borg

Change Your Life with CBT by Corinne Sweet

Change Your Thinking - Change Your Life by Brian Tracy

Happiness by Richard Layard

Learned Optimism by Martin Seligman

The A - Z of Good Mental Health by Jeremy Thomas and Dr Tony Hughes

Wet Mind: The New Cognitive Neuroscience by Stephen Michael Kosslyn and Olivier Koenig

Other Books by Liggy Webb

Resilience - How to cope when everything keeps changing
How to Be Happy - Simple ways to be happier and healthier
How to Work Wonders - Your Guide to Workplace Wellness
Thank You - Your Guide to Appreciating Life

Global Corporate Challenge

The Global Corporate Challenge is an excellent opportunity to integrate behavior changes in your workplace and do something that I believe every individual and business would benefit from getting involved in. We need to get the world moving, healthy and energised and this is a fantastic initiative. Even just by starting slowly, getting active will make a huge difference to your overall individual health and happiness but is also proven to add value to business.

The Global Corporate Challenge® (GCC) is the world's largest and most exciting workplace health initiative that empowers its participants to become active within their day to day lives via simple and sustainable changes - motivated by teamwork, goal setting and a virtual journey around the world.

Starting in May each year, the GCC takes participants on a 16 week virtual walking journey around the world and engages and supports them to become more active by aiming to take 10,000 steps a day – three times more than the average office worker walks in a day. Accessible to every staff member regardless of location, age or base fitness level, the GCC's success is its science-based approach that creates genuine, long-term behavioural change.

The remarkable results from a study conducted by the Foundation for Chronic Disease Prevention in the Workplace (FCDP) demonstrated significant improvements in energy levels, enhanced enjoyment of day to day activities, increases in overall confidence levels, self-esteem, ability to handle stress and importantly a higher level of general happiness and wellbeing.

For more details around the proven benefits you can receive by participating visit

www.chronicdiseaseprevention.org or to find out how to get your workplace involved in the GCC, visit www.gettheworld moving.com

TEAM TONIC

Coming together is a beginning.
Keeping together is progress.
Working together is success.
Henry Ford

Team Tonic is an engaging and highly interactive, one-day personal and team development event. It aims to energise teams and develop positive skills and behaviours through sustainable learning as devised by The MotivAction Group in conjunction with Liggy Webb and The Learning Architect.

This high impact event helps to support culture shift and workplace change, embed new values, replace bad habits with good ones, and boost performance and wellness at work.

Delivered by expert facilitators, and based on a blended and sustainable learning approach, *Team Tonic* is a proven and straightforward way to inform, energise and inspire your team.

How does it work?

Team Tonic events are tailored to meet your change management, performance improvement and organisational development needs.

The interactive morning workshop incorporates team energisers, and two 60-minute Modern Life Skills personal development sessions.

The development sessions provide sustainable learning based on the UNESCO model and each session includes personal action planning time. Ongoing post-event support is provided to ensure sustainable learning.

Choose two of the 20 key life skills covered in this book to be delivered as one hour bite size sessions designed to develop positive and adaptive behaviours.

The afternoon session focuses on team building and development, and includes a 90-minute facilitated team activity, such as:

The Bigger Picture

Encourages networking and cross team working in the creation of a bespoke work of art that reflects your key messages and team objectives, providing a lasting image for ongoing communications.

Bridging the Gap

Highlights team work, excellent customer service, communication, understanding requirements, sharing best practices and delivering on time.

Chain Reaction

Focuses on great intra- and inter-team working, combating 'silo mentality' and sharing a one-team ethos.

Connexions

Highlights the importance of improved communication and the sharing of accurate data and best practices across teams, departments and different locations.

A facilitated half-day follow-up session is provided three to six months after each *Team Tonic* event to review individual action plans and team development objectives.

Who is it suitable for?

- Any business or organisation that is preparing for or undergoing significant change.
- Any business or organisation wanting to boost motivation, positive behavioural skills, and individual or team performance.
- Any business looking to improve workplace wellness and morale.
- All ages, genders, grades and backgrounds.

What are the benefits and outcomes?

- Encourages positive attitudes and adaptive behaviours.
- Enables individuals to take personal responsibility.
- Supports culture shift and changing mindsets, replacing bad habits with good ones.
- Sustainable learning and change through personal action plans and post-event support.
- Promotes performance improvement and motivation.
- Improved team working and communication.
- Improved client focus and customer care.

For further information contact The MotivAction Group at teamtonic@motivaction.co.uk or call 01438 861494.

© 2012 The MotivAction Group www.motivaction.co.uk

About the Author

Liggy Webb is widely respected as a leading expert in the field of Modern Life Skills. As a presenter, consultant and author she is passionate about her work and improving the quality of people's lives.

Liggy is noted for her dynamic and engaging style and as a result is frequently invited to present and speak at international conferences, award ceremonies, on board cruise ships, in the media and at a variety of high profile events.

Liggy has quite an eclectic range of experience. Having worked in the learning and development arena for over twenty years she is the founding director of The Learning Architect, a consortium of behavioural skills specialists.

www.thelearningarchitect.com

As an international consultant for The United Nations Liggy travels extensively to various duty stations and peace missions around the world. She describes her visit to Afghanistan in 2011 as her most interesting and enlightening experience to date.

She is passionate about supporting mental health charities and is a trustee of The Chrysalis Foundation a development programme that engages, inspires and compels offenders to make a sustainable change in their lives.